AMERICAN GIRL LIBRARY

The American Girl Book
of Teen-Age Questions

Do you occasionally come up against problems too big for you to handle? Does it seem impossible to live up to your dreams of the kind of person you'd like to be? Do your parents seem to resist every move you make toward growing up? Are your sisters and brothers so irritating at times that you could scream?

Cheer up! You are not alone; and you'll find the answers to these and countless other questions in this book, whose purpose is to help you on the way to becoming a responsible, happy, and well-adjusted woman.

The American Girl Book of TEEN-AGE QUESTIONS

With answers by Nancy Davies, *American Girl* Magazine's
"What's on Your Mind?" columnist

Illustrations by Stan Phillips

RANDOM HOUSE   NEW YORK

Contents

Foreword

Coming of age, the process of growing up from a little girl to a full-fledged adult, is one of the most challenging but also one of the most difficult tasks in life. Fortunately it doesn't happen overnight and there is lots of fun and excitement along the way. But along with the fun there are all sorts of decisions to be faced, questions to be answered that add up to the one big problem that girls have in common: growing up!

How can I learn to understand myself?

How can I understand my parents better and persuade them to understand me?

How can I develop a personality of my own and at the same time be a popular member of my group?

How do I decide what vocation I am best suited for?

How do I go about establishing the right kind of friendships with boys?

How do I achieve a mature attitude about getting along with people?

These are some of the big questions everybody has to wrestle with during the growing-up years, but happily nobody has to do it all alone. There is always help if you know where to look for it and that is where this book comes in. Here you will find many questions and their carefully considered answers taken from the monthly column "What's on Your Mind?" which appears in *The American Girl* Magazine. These questions have been asked of columnist Nancy Davies by girls like you all over the world. Among them you will surely find questions you have been asking yourself with many of the answers you have been looking for.

ESTHER R. BIEN, EDITOR
The American Girl Magazine

The American Girl Book
of Teen-Age Questions

My Problem Is . . .
Myself

Chapter 1

You want to be loved, admired and respected for your own very special qualities, the ones that make you just a little different from everybody else in the world. You'd like to be the kind of person who is popular for many reasons, whose ideas and opinions other people value. To be what you'd like best to be, you want to look as attractive as you possibly can; you want your personality to shine like a star, and you want the kind of self-confidence which makes you do and say the right things at the right time.

The questions and answers in this chapter

cover many of the problems which girls who want the same things you do have been troubled about. Look them over and see whether one or more of them will help you be the girl of your dreams.

Q Something is wrong with me, but I can't find out what it is. All the kids at school seem to hate me. They call me all kinds of names, like "mule" and "baboon." They try to trip me as I go down the aisle. They talk and whisper about me right in front of me. Nothing's bad about me physically, that I can see. I try all the good-grooming, better personality, and good-manners suggestions in magazine articles. I haven't a good friend who could set me right. I would value any suggestions you have to offer.
RITA, AGE 13, OKLAHOMA

A It may very well be, Rita, that about the only thing "wrong" with you is that you're easily teased. It's a strange thing, but once a group (like this classroom of children) finds a sensitive, timid member they delight in ganging up on that person. When they see that you cannot be teased, they will stop. Try your best to laugh with them and be friendly. This will be hard to do, but it's the only cure.

In addition to trying to be a little thicker-skinned, and ignoring their rude behavior, it would be a good idea to get some help from your teacher on how to make friends. Talk to her alone some day, not to tattle on the others, but to ask her if she can think of things you might do to be better liked. It may be that she has noticed you feel lonely, but has hesitated to say anything for fear of hurting your feelings.

Q **I like boys a lot,** at least I think I do. But when I find a boy friend I like him only a few weeks, and then break up with him. The only boy I liked for a long time moved away. I do hope you can help me understand myself better. VALERIE, AGE 14, ARIZONA

A **The fickleness which puzzles you, Valerie,** is the most normal reaction imaginable. This frequent switching of interest is really nature's way of helping you get acquainted with a wide variety of personalities, so that later on, when the time comes for serious consideration of a lifetime partner, you'll have arrived at some judgments that will serve you well.

It works the same way with boys this age. When a boy who has seemed to like a certain girl a lot suddenly "drops" her, it doesn't mean that something is mysteriously "wrong" with her. He's merely responding to that natural instinct to widen his range of acquaintances.

Q **There are so many things** that I don't understand about growing up that I am unable to express my feelings. Though I have many friends, I can't talk to them, or to my mother. All I do when I feel terribly mixed up is go to my room, or go for a walk and talk to myself. Is there anything wrong with this? Some people say that your teen-age years are the best, but I don't agree. When I get confused I wish I could be a tiny child again.
MARY, AGE 15, KANSAS

A   You aren't alone in finding it hard to grow up, Mary. Everyone, to some extent, has this frightened feeling about taking on the responsibilities of being grown up. I'd feel sorry for anyone who really expected their teen-age years to be the best, wouldn't you? What would there be to look forward to? But to try to fall back on childhood, instead of looking ahead, would be even more foolish.

There's nothing wrong in wanting to be alone, sometimes, to think things out, but it's also sensible to try to learn how others have solved the problems of growing up. There are fascinating books about how girls have struggled to find themselves. Two you might try, almost sure to be in your library, are "The Young Brontés" by Mary L. Jarden and "Yours With Love, Kate," by Miriam E. Mason. Both are about real girls who became writers. Your librarian or your English teacher will also be glad to tell you of others that may throw some light on your problems.

You say you have many friends. Among them there must be girls, or at least *one* girl, who has a need to share her mixed-up feel-

ings, and who would love to have you ask her
to go walking and talk over some of the things
that bother you. Often, two people can think
things out better than either one can by mud-
dling along alone.

Q **I get jealous very easily.** I try to overcome it but can't. I have a wonderful family
and many friends, and the most wonderful
boy friend a girl could have. But when one of
my friends gets something new or something
good happens to her, I get jealous. My mother
feels happy for her, but I feel slighted. They
say you shouldn't have the same boy friend
too long, but I can't give up mine, because I
like him too much and don't want anyone
else to have him. I try so hard not to be this
way, but I'm still the same. Please try to help
me. Lois, Age 13, Ohio

A **You are really describing** two traits, Lois
—envy and jealousy—and both are exceed-
ingly unpleasant qualities.

When one is jealous, it is because one wants
the special, single-minded devotion of another

person. This is like the demanding love of a baby. But a grownup is more sensible and wants to *share* friends, possessions, thoughts, and feelings.

Envy is an ugly feeling. It means that one is resentful of the good fortune of others. Again, it reflects a childish wish to be on the receiving end of all good things.

The very fact that you are trying to do away with mean feelings indicates that you haven't strayed too far in the wrong direction. Just being aware of the situation means that you've already taken a big step.

Now is the time to start on the next step— that is, to make a conscious effort to overcome these traits. When you find yourself feeling jealous or envious, just stop and think about it at that *very* moment. Use your own common sense and some good, clear thinking to talk yourself out of such feelings. For example, the fact that a good thing is happening to someone else does not mean that something bad is happening to you, nor does it mean that you won't ever have a similarly pleasant experience.

I suspect that you've been giving way to your feelings a little too easily, instead of really trying to overcome them with concrete facts. With this kind of effort, you will gradually grow into the kind of person you want to be.

Q **Whenever someone asks me** over to her house for the night I usually accept, but within an hour or so I wish I hadn't. Wherever I go I get homesick. I've never been to a summer camp, and I have no desire to go. I hate to turn people down; but I don't really care even to have people sleep at my house. What should I do? Louise, Age 12, Pennsylvania

A **Without knowing anything** about your home life, Louise, it's very hard to make a guess as to why you shy away from close contacts outside your family circle. And I can't tell if having friends stay over bothers you because it encourages return invitations or if you find the situation awkward for some other reason. In any case, it may help you to know that preferring to be alone and being home-sick are feelings that most people experience when they first begin to separate themselves from their childhood ways of clinging to parents. Staying close to home seems very comforting, indeed, when you're uneasy about trying out your own wings. But try you must —or you'll never learn to fly! Get used to being away from home a little at a time now, so you won't miss out on a lot of fun later—when you may have the chance to go away to camp, on week-end trips, and eventually even to college. You mention that you usually accept overnight invitations. The next step is not to let the fact that you regret going get in your way. Concentrate on being a good guest. The more you interest yourself in others and participate in the activities around you, the sooner you'll begin to enjoy yourself—and, gradually, instead of feeling homesick when you visit, you'll find it hard to tear yourself away from all the fun.

Q **My problem has been bothering me a long time.** My mother says I will outgrow it, but I haven't yet. I am so self-conscious that I'm even afraid to ask a question in class, for fear it's already been asked, though I've paid attention. I won't get up in front of the class to give a speech or a report. With my close friends, I'm all right; but inside a classroom, among kids I don't know too well, everything goes wrong. My friends don't seem to experience this problem. Is it common for girls of my age? How can I overcome it? SUE, AGE 14, CALIFORNIA

A   It's very common, Sue, though not always to the degree that it bothers you. The important thing, for you, is to start the climb toward confidence as soon as possible.

Next time a question is asked in class and you are *sure* of the answer, take a deep breath and raise your hand. Once you've had this fraction of success, each time you make a contribution you will worry less about stumbling in front of the others, and will add to your belief in yourself. Since you say it isn't difficult for you to speak with people you know well, perhaps getting to know your classmates better would help, too. Take advantage of class breaks and lunch hours to mingle with them and see if it doesn't make it easier to face them as a group.

Many schools have speech classes for students like you who are shy about speaking in front of a group. If you have such a program in your school, ask to be admitted to a class. The teacher will be someone trained especially to make things as easy for you as possible. Your fellow students will very likely be people who have the same troubles you have. If you fumble sometimes, they won't laugh, and neither will the teacher. By the end of the year you may find yourself on the debating team. At the very least, you'll find that you can express yourself as easily to people you don't know well as you can to your friends.

Q Although I was very popular and had many friends last year, things have changed. Just recently one of my girl friends has become very popular. I don't really mind taking second place, but I seem to be losing all my self-confidence. I keep finding things that are wrong with myself and am even beginning to believe that my friends don't like me. I don't understand it at all. Please help, for I'm desperate. BETTY, AGE 14, DISTRICT OF COLUMBIA.

A   As I see it, Betty, your problem is a mixture of two things. One is that popularity isn't a stable, permanent affair. The kind of "popularity" you speak of is a come-and-go business, and the realization that there will be ups and downs should keep you from taking them too seriously.

The other half of the problem has to do with the kind of self-scrutiny that can help or harm a person. Looking at yourself questioningly is fine, for we all want to improve ourselves. But making a concentrated effort to pick faults with yourself can end in hopeless discouragement. Try instead to be friendly and cheerful, and a good sport. These are the qualities that form the basis for really worthwhile popularity. And last, I can't resist repeating an old, but true, cliché: we can't all be first. If you think about it, I'm sure you'll admit that being in what you call "second place" for a while is really not so terrible at that.

Q **I am twelve, and getting interested** in boys. But the boys don't exactly consider me a girl! You see, the boys in our school have always known me as a tomboy—which I still am and may be for a long while. None of them pays much attention to me except when we are playing, or talking about sports, or when they want some advice. Advice seems to be my specialty. The boys ask me about a girl, what she's like, what section she's in, if she has a boy friend, etc. Please tell me how I can convince the boys that I am really a girl.
SUE, AGE 12, PENNSYLVANIA

A **What a lucky girl you are!** I can't think of a nicer relationship between boys and girls your age than the one you describe. Think of all the girls who are so shy they can't think of a way to get boys to talk with them. The comfortable companionship you have now will help you make conversation and feel at ease someday—when you become romantically interested in a boy.

Meanwhile, if you want to be thought of as a girl, you'll have to accept the fact that it won't happen until you gradually soften your outward ways. Be interested in sports, but move away from playing rough-and-tumble games. Begin learning how to walk and sit gracefully. Take a look at yourself and see if a new hairdo is in order. Open your closet and try putting together some new wardrobe combinations for school. Continue talking to the boys about the same things as in the past, but stop using slang phrases or words of comradeship that are popular among boys. Don't expect a miracle overnight, Sue, especially among the boys you've known for some time. But if you follow along these lines, I guarantee there will be a difference.

Q   **When some little thing comes up,** and I can't have my way, I let go with my loud, crazy temper. Just the other day I wanted to go to a certain movie and Mom didn't want me to, so I cried and carried on terribly.

I've tried everything I can think of to cure my bad temper, but nothing works. Have you any ideas?

CAROL, AGE 12, KENTUCKY

A   **You're already on your way** to conquering that temper, Carol, though you may not know it. Now that you've recognized the childishness of such explosions, and really *think* about your behavior as a problem, you're passing into a do-something-about-it stage.

Have the methods you've tried taken account of the fact that when you get angry your body manufactures energy to help you get out of your predicament? But yelling and screaming aren't productive ways of using that energy! A harmless way of getting rid of the "mad" state would be to race out of the house, sweep the porch, rake leaves, climb a tree—anything that would let off all that extra steam. If you can't go out-of-doors, dash to your room and try doing something physical

—such as the most difficult setting-up exercise you know, or brushing your hair fiercely. I'll wager that once you're away from other people you won't feel like shrieking, and you may even find yourself laughing.

Once you can laugh, or even smile, you're taking a giant step toward understanding the difference between things worth getting angry about and those so petty you'll be reluctant to let them get the better of you.

Q **Although I'm pretty popular with girls** when I go to school parties, the boys never seem to notice me. My best girl friend can talk to boys, but I am too self-conscious to. I am very tall and have lots of freckles, and for a long time I thought this was the reason boys paid no attention to me. But now I think the real reason is that I'm sort of shy and stupid around boys. I want to be an artist, and my mother says I can go away to a school where there are art classes, as there aren't here. Maybe if I could start all over and make new friends, things would be better. I feel so uncertain over whether I should stay here and compete with my girl friends or go to a boarding school. KATHY, AGE 15, MISSOURI

A   It is a little difficult to talk to boys at first, but with practice, it gets easier. Try to meet them halfway; smile and say hello; ask about their interests; tell them about your own activities—what happened to you during the day, your favorite things to eat, sports, and so on; talk about the decorations at the party; try to join your friends and have fun in a group; and learn to dress so that you bring out your best features. Being tall enables you to wear many styles becomingly, so take advantage of it.

Changing schools is another matter. In the long run, you and your parents are the ones to make that decision. One trouble, though, with starting all over in a strange city is that it places you in a new school where you'd hardly be in a position to "compete" any better than at home. It may be a good idea to put off your plans for art school until you reach college age, and concentrate meanwhile on building up your self-confidence.

Q **I am quite cute,** and have many friends. But all the girls and some of the boys make fun of me because I won't neck. I think we're too young. My very best girl friend is quite popular with the boys since they found out she will neck with them. I think it is really kind of silly. When the boys come over to my house I just put on a stack of records and we dance. But I feel they just think I'm being queer, for they end up going over to my friend's house. I was always told by my parents that a boy respects a girl more if she says no when he wants to kiss, and I've believed this. But now I don't know. Am I the one who's being silly? Please help! CATHY, AGE 13, MISSOURI

A **Silly? You're being sharp!** If you did lose a boy friend because of the standards you set for yourself, good riddance! Your real boy friends will like you for your individual qualities and understand you as a person. Go right on believing in your parents and trusting in their and in your own judgment.

The time will come, someday, when you know a boy well and are truly fond of him, that you'll want to show your affection with a kiss. Perhaps on a birthday, or as congratulations for a success, or when leaving on vacation, or as a simple thank-you—but the kiss will be bestowed in a friendly way; never as a means of entertainment, and never if you don't want to.

Q **A very good friend** has had me over any number of times to spend the night, but I can't bring myself to invite her back. I'm afraid she won't enjoy it. Her house is larger and has TV in three rooms, her parents are quiet and reserved, and it's always so peaceful there. My home is the exact opposite; I have two small sisters, a big brother, and two very friendly parents. We have only one TV and there's always an argument. I love all my family very much, but I'm afraid my friend would never want to come back.
JANIE, AGE 13, WEST VIRGINIA

A **Your house sounds so much livelier** and jollier, Janie, that I hate to think of what your friend's been missing! Most only children yearn for the companionship of a big family, including arguments that sometimes raise the roof.

Most of us have a silly tendency to think we know how our friends will react when visiting us. We fret about appearances, lacks of one sort or another. We apologize for differences, forgetting that people like the novelty of differences. You're denying your friend a new kind of enjoyment by not letting her spend a night under the roof of your friendly and welcoming parents. Invite her and she will sincerely thank you for a wonderful time.

Q **This is a really big problem to us.** We are the only girls in our school, it seems, who like classical music, ballet, and so on, so the others, both boys and girls, laugh at us to our faces and talk about us behind our backs.

It's not as if we keep talking a lot about our interests, but still we're considered "different." We are even told this will affect our future popularity. What puzzles us is that we always read about how people like you better if you are "yourself," but this doesn't seem to work in our case.

CINDY AND DEBBY, AGE 12, OKLAHOMA

A   You two girls are up against a situation many others face, too. Just think of all the boys and girls who are considered "different" because they don't like sports or because they do like poetry! The fact of the matter is we're all "different"—and a good thing, too. It's just that sometimes we are different in less noticeable ways. But wouldn't it be pretty dull if we knew only people who thought exactly as we did?

Certainly it's never any fun to be in a situation where your particular preferences, be they musical or otherwise, are made fun of. It sounds as though your classmates may not yet understand the importance of tolerating the views of others. Try not to let their teasing get you down. Perhaps if they feel you are interested in listening to them about their likes and dislikes, even though you may not agree, they'll be less likely to mock your tastes.

The ability to respect others' opinions in the

way that you want yours to be respected, and the courage to be yourself, are lifelong qualities that will, in the long run, earn you many worth-while friends.

Q **I would like to know** the right and wrong places for wearing shorts. I don't mind wearing them to the swimming pool or around the house, but I don't think it is correct to wear them to the store, library, etc. Thank you for considering my problem.
MARY, AGE 12, ILLINOIS

A **You might take this** as a general rule, Mary: The larger the community in which you live, the fewer places there are where it is considered good form to wear shorts. In other words, the more "public" there is around, the more careful you have to be about how you dress.

For example, your illustrations of the swimming pool and the library are good. At the swimming pool, you are likely to be among other people your own age, who all dress somewhat alike. At the library, you will be meeting people of all ages, some of whom have strict ideas about what is proper. So if you want to appear at your best, it's well to take others' feelings into consideration and not to dress in ways that call attention to yourself.

In your suburb, I feel sure that no one would criticize you for running to a neighborhood store in shorts, provided you aren't so fat, or so tall, or so striking, that shorts make you look ridiculous. On a big-city street, however, such informal dress would be taboo.

Q **What shall I do?** The friend with whom I go on dates, to dances, movies, and so on, is many inches shorter than I am. I wear flats, but it doesn't seem to help any. I don't wear a high hairdo, either. I look simply terrible. Please help. PATTY, AGE 15, NEW YORK

A **At your age, Patty,** a girl doesn't usually grow much any more. Not so with a boy. His height is still highly unpredictable at this age. Since he may not yet have reached his full height he may catch up to, and top, you before you can turn around. But it would be a sad day if every girl accepted invitations only from boys as tall or taller than herself.

I'm sure you *don't* look terrible. You'll feel less conspicuous if you stop imagining that people are noticing the difference in height between you and your escort. You've been quick to think of such things as low heels and hairdo, now just think of being a lot of fun.

Remember, too, that some of the happiest marriages would never have taken place if the girls had measured love by inches!

Q **I am fifteen** and one of my main troubles is my weight. Any girl who is five feet five and weighs 153 pounds has a big problem. In seven or eight months I've gone to three doctors and have lost only one pound. Yes, it's true! Though I've stayed on a strict diet I can't seem to lose, and it has made me so shy and quiet I haven't a friend. What can I do to make at least a few friends? My mother and I are the only ones at home, and it gets pretty lonesome with no one my own age to talk to or go places with. CONNIE, AGE 15, OHIO

A   It is indeed hard to understand why following doctor's orders hasn't resulted in any noticeable weight loss. There is one other thing you could do that might help. That is, to check with a chart the number of calories in the amount of food you eat, and thus discover whether you're unknowingly eating more than you should.

Such a list may be had for five cents from: Superintendent of Documents, Government Printing Office, Washington 25, D.C. Ask for Agriculture Information Bulletin No. 36, "Food Values in Common Portions." This is a valuable list for anyone because it shows how to get the best nutrition without piling up unwanted calories. Maybe you've been eating just slightly bigger portions of some foods than you should. Perhaps on this list you'll find foods that you like that are permissible and are less weight-threatening than you imagine. I feel confident that your doctor will encourage you in this approach, but do consult with him again.

As for having friends, Connie, you can't possibly make them if you avoid contacts. I know it's much easier to say, "Join in" than to do so, but unless you take *some* part in school or church activities you're deliberately making your problem worse. Clubs or groups that encourage physical exercise would be excellent—swimming, bird-watching hikes, bowling, folk dancing are all such fun.

It will take a big effort. But keep in mind that every girl you know has difficulties to overcome, though their problems may not be outwardly obvious, as yours is.

Q **Last year I began** to have a nicely rounded bust, but now my right breast is one and a half inches larger than my left. When I buy a new bra I have to sew tucks in it or stuff in facial tissues. Even then, I think the girls whisper behind my back, which is very embarrassing. I really do need help.
MARGIE, AGE 12, ALASKA

A **Too bad you've been worrying, Margie,** for nothing's the matter. It's human nature to be sensitive about one's body during the years in which great changes are going on. While one's figure is developing, it's common for growth to be lopsided. Any time now you may find that the difference between your breasts is lessening and that it will presently disappear. Meanwhile, until you even out, just keep on adjusting your bra.

Q **I'm becoming more and more troubled** by my problem. Whenever I go to a party I get flustered and hot, and begin to perspire to an embarrassing extent. My dress stains and then I sort of fade into the background. I bathe every day, am especially careful to use deodorant. But it happens whenever I want to be enjoying myself—even in gym. Everyone tries to be nice to me, but there's an uncomfortable feeling on my friends' part, as well as my own. Please help! I'm desperate!
CAROL, AGE 14, MARYLAND

A **Worry and fear may be causing** part of your trouble. You mention trying to be relaxed and calm (I've had to cut your letter down), so it's obvious that you recognize the connection between one's feelings and the body's glandular behavior. But even taking into account the fact that some people perspire more than others, there may be an explanation and a remedy for your excessive perspiring. Your doctor is the person to go to. Do not hesitate to do this. If he decides there may be some glandular imbalance, he will try to correct it.

Meanwhile, you might try an antiperspirant and use dress shields in your clothing and your gym suit.

Q Can you tell me something to do about bad breath? I have tried gargles, tooth paste, and all sorts of things, but I keep on being embarrassed by it. The other day a boy even spoke to me about it. I'm afraid I'll never have dates until I do something about this.
MARGARET, AGE 14, ILLINOIS

A This is really a health problem, Margaret, but it has become a psychological problem to you, so it is appropriate for this page.

The remedies you have tried weren't very helpful because mouth washes and such things

don't get at the deep-down *cause* of bad breath
—they only cover it up for the time being. Are
your teeth in good condition? If you haven't
had them cleaned within the last six months,
that's the first thing to have done, for your
dentist may uncover trouble. If your teeth
turn out to be all right, an examination by
your doctor or the school doctor would be
next in order. Your diet and your health habits in general may need to be checked, and
only a physician can do this. Trying remedies
that have worked for others is foolish; your
health is too precious to risk. You mustn't go
on being bothered by something that can be
corrected with proper treatment.

Q   I could just cry—and do! I'm completely
flat-chested and at my age it's inexcusable.
I'm never asked for a date, although I'm well
enough liked by girls. Added to my figure
problem is that I have a twenty-three inch
waistline and absolutely no hips, which makes
my waist look thirty inches. Can I do anything about these two problems?
JENNY, AGE 16, DELAWARE

A   Body build is one of the few things we can't do very much about. Even though we can't alter our height, or the size of our feet, there are advantages about most of these disconcerting features that gradually come to our attention. For instance, the tall girl finds she can wear clothes that make her the envy of the broadly built, short girl. You may not develop much of a bust, but you can always fall back on padded bras to disguise the lack in front.

For all-over body balance nothing can beat swimming. Exercises, tennis, basketball, will also help give you that supple, graceful look.

If you are an interesting girl, Jenny, full of fun, a good companion, and well-groomed, the dates will come, never fear.

Q   Is it polite to refuse food when I'm on a date? I'm on the heavy side, so I watch my weight and try not to eat anything that would make me gain. But when I'm on a date and go for pizza or ice cream, I don't know what to say. My boy friend doesn't think I'm fat. How can I watch what I eat and yet turn him down politely? TERRY, AGE 14, PENNSYLVANIA

A When you say you're on the heavy side, Terry, have you taken into consideration such important factors as your build, whether you are large- or small-boned, and how your weight is distributed?

However, if you tend to gain quickly when you eat sweets and between-meal snacks, you're smart to stay away from those extra tidbits. You can make your refusal painless to both you and your date by sticking to sherberts, tomato juice, or other low-calorie dishes. Sometimes, too, when you suspect the evening's plans might include pizza, you could have a low-calorie dinner, and then safely go a tiny bit overboard on a snack later.

Q Maybe other girls don't have my problem. I hate to take my clothes off for a checkup at the doctor's. I just can't do it. I'm really desperate, so please help me.
CHRISTINE, AGE 11, UTAH

A **Other girls** *do* feel as you do; sometimes they even refuse invitations to stay with friends overnight because they are used to complete privacy while undressing.

What is troubling you is a sort of false modesty. You are putting too much emphasis on something that is entirely matter-of-course to a physician. Your doctor looks at your skin because it tells him a good deal about your health—about whether you're eating the right foods for instance.

How in the world does this embarrassed feeling come to pester girls so? Mostly because they are taught, from the time they can first remember, to be modest. But to be ashamed of one's body is quite another thing.

Of course, there are girls who go to the opposite extreme, who dress in a way that can really be called immodest because they want to attract attention. But there's a happy medium between flaunting what might otherwise be a graceful figure and hiding behind one's clothing as if it were a disguise.

Since you're just at the turning point between little girlhood and adolescence, Christine, you haven't "lived with" the "new" body you've been acquiring long enough to feel comfortable with it. Your doctor understands your feelings, you may be sure, and he'll make your checkups as easy for you as he can.

Q **I haven't ever been asked** to go on a date, and I think it's because I have to wear glasses. My relatives say I look very well in them, but I think it's just to make me feel less self-conscious about wearing them.

My friend told me that one of her teachers told her class that "Men seldom make passes at girls who wear glasses." This hurt me very much, and made me even more self-conscious than before. What can I do?
CECELIA, AGE 14, NEW YORK

A **Because a famous rhymester** like Dorothy Parker once happened to write a couplet based on girls' self-consciousness is a very. far-fetched reason for you to worry, Cecelia. Whether or not you wear glasses has nothing to do with your popularity. If there's any truth in the rhyme, it applies to girls who never for a minute forget they have specs on. Boys take a shine to girls who act natural, who are not wrapped up in a cocoon of fear that they may not be attractive.

Instead of focusing on your glasses—and yourself—look at the world around you. Many a pair of glasses has enhanced the wearer's appearance. Especially nowadays, with the gay, colorful variety in which frames come, the right ones can blend right in with a pert expression that says, "I'm interested in you, not myself!" What really counts is good grooming and an attractive personality.

Q **I'd like to know, once and for all,** whether there's any truth in the old wives' tale that it's harmful during menstruation to wash your hair and take baths.

I've just begun, too, to want to take a daily bath so that there'll be no question about my personal freshness. My parents seem to think that a fast washing morning and night is all that is required each day, and that taking a bath every day of the week is unnecessary. How about it? PAT, AGE 13, NEW YORK

A   How long it takes for traditional beliefs to die out! I suspect that the idea of baths being harmful came about while houses were still so poorly heated that chilling after a bath could easily take place. In those far-off days, too, much less was known about physical health and disease prevention. Dirt is a harborer of all kinds of enemies to health, even when it's not obvious dirt that "shows" on one's skin. A daily warm bath is a protection against trouble, whether or not one is going through the menstrual period. As for shampooing your hair, make sure it's thoroughly dry before you go outside.

Q   My problem is that I have black rings below my eyes. I've tried everything in this world to get rid of them, but nothing helps. It's embarrassing when my friends ask what they are, and I have to tell them I don't know. Please help! LINDA, AGE 14, MINNESOTA

A   When you say you've tried "every-thing," Linda, does this include your family doctor—asking and following his advice about health rules, proper sleep, and diet? If so, and you have no health or skin problems, then you may be one of those people for whom this condition seems to be natural.

If your doctor and your mother okay the idea, there are a number of cosmetics available that will mask this condition for special occasions.

My Problem Is . . .
My Family

Chapter 2

At some time during her growing years, every girl has trouble getting along with the family. Most often it's parents. Frequently it's brothers or sisters.

Keep in mind, when you read this chapter to see whether your problem is discussed, that your parents also have problems which have to be solved, in areas which don't involve you at all.

Unless you ask for help, they may not even know you need it since they are naturally busy with interests of their own. (Luckily for you! Who wants parents watching every move she makes?)

Failure to get coöperation from your parents when you *do* ask often means that they are concerned less with your present pleasure than with the many years of life ahead of you. However grown-up you feel, they know that your experience is limited. They are imposing on you some of the disciplines you will have to impose on yourself as you become independent of them.

Sometimes it is hard for parents to recognize that you are growing up and need to widen your horizons, stand on your own feet, make your own decisions, develop a personality of your own. If you understand this and go about changing their attitude in the right way, then it will make your relationship a much happier one and do much to convince them that you really are as grown-up as you think you are.

Brothers and sisters whom you really love can cause friction, too. Learning to play fair, to conquer jealousy, to respect their differing personalities and viewpoints, their privacy and possessions, to take an interest in their problems, and to give them affectionate understanding, will make life pleasant at home and help to give you that valuable asset—the ability to get along well with others.

Q When I go to friends' houses overnight they always seem *so* close to their mothers and fathers. At home, it is different. I don't feel free to kiss my parents or to talk over serious or personal problems with them. I love my mother and father and think they're the best in the world, but why can't I feel free with them, as my friends are with their parents? PAM, AGE 12, OHIO

A If you had a wider circle of friends, Pam, you'd be sure to run into families that are as reserved as yours is. It's simply a matter of upbringing and habit that enables some parents to show their affection very openly, and others to be less demonstrative. Your parents' love of you is just as deep and warm, I'm confident, as that of people who are less restrained in their expressions of affection—

otherwise you wouldn't say your father and mother are "the best in the world."

It's more than likely that your parents would welcome occasional signs of affection on your part. They may realize that they are a little inhibited in their ability to be lavish in such expressions. As for not feeling free to talk things over with them, why not take the plunge and assume that they would be happy to have you confide in them? Many parents hesitate to intrude on the inner thoughts and feelings of their children. Yours may seem to be cold when, actually, it's shyness that keeps them from seeking to share your secrets.

Q A while back I went with a boy to a dance. When he came to pick me up, my parents told him to bring me home right after the dance. We stopped at a place for a sandwich and Coke after the dance, and my parents were upset and angry because he hadn't brought me home immediately. Now they say that before I can go out with a boy, he must talk to them. I am beginning to worry that boys will not ask me out any more because they're all afraid to talk to my mother and father. CHRISTINE, AGE 14, OHIO

A **Are you perhaps frightening** the boys off yourself by implying that they will be pounced upon with a lecture? Don't your parents really just want an opportunity to tell a boy when you should be home? It is customary for a young man to reassure the parents of the girl he takes out of her safety while in his company. A boy who isn't grown-up enough to realize this is not old enough to be entrusted with you for an evening.

As for your part in the situation, you know that it takes two to stop for a sandwich and Coke. It is up to you to be home on time and to remind the boy—if he has forgotten—when you must go. If you really take this responsibility into your own hands, your parents will ease their restrictions. I think you should talk to your mother and father, assure them of your reliability, and ask them not to base their judgments on one unfortunate evening. Then live up to your word.

Q **This may sound selfish,** but ever since I can remember I have wanted a room by my-self. I've talked with my parents about it, but they don't agree with me at all. My dad is building another master bedroom and a den and playroom, and it will leave an empty bedroom. I don't like nursery rhymes on my wall like my sister; I would like one small room to be the way I want it. Please help.
JANE, AGE 11, CALIFORNIA

A **It is not selfish** to want a room of your own. Every girl needs a certain amount of privacy when she is approaching or is in her teens. You're not to blame for having out-grown nursery rhymes or wishing for that small extra bedroom. Your mother is likely to understand how you feel—do try talking to her again. Assure your parents that you would take care of the room and keep it neat. You might also suggest that they read pages 112–

166 of "Parents' Questions" by staff members
of the Child Study Association (Harpers, Rev.
Edition, 1947) or pages 25, 32, and 50 of "The
Adolescent in Your Family," a pamphlet they
can obtain free of charge from the Children's
Bureau, Dept. of Health, Education, and
Welfare, Washington 25, D.C.

Q **My parents repeat things** I say about
people that I don't want them to repeat. They
even tell the person what I've said when I'm
right there. My remarks aren't bad or mean,
but when I explain that it's embarrassing,
they only laugh. Sometimes I wonder if they
really love me, or why would they be doing
this to me? I love them, but I don't know
what to do about it. KAREN, AGE 13, IDAHO

A **It's not that your parents** don't love you,
Karen. It's probable they haven't fully realized how much the process of growing up has
changed your thoughts and feelings. Most
people repeat funny things that children say
because they show, in an amusing way, how
inexperienced a child is. But later, a young

person becomes sensitive about being quoted. Your parents don't yet realize that a thirteen-year-old like yourself is mature enough to care not to be embarrassed.

For a while, it might be a good idea not to say things about people that you do not wish to have repeated. Don't go overboard by keeping everything to yourself, but do try it in instances that are particularly important.

Here's another approach that has worked for others. The next time your remarks are repeated, try not to close up tight as an oyster. Remember that your parents don't mean to humiliate you; they just can't believe you are adult in your conversation. On occasion, you might even add to the comments, explaining why you thought this, or how you observed that. Conversation would improve all around, and I think that in time your parents would gradually forget their habit, leaving you to speak your own words.

Q **Maybe my problem is shared** by many girls, maybe not, but it troubles me terribly.

By parents think I am boy crazy. My point of view is that of course I like certain boys and have my crushes. I talk about boys at home to a certain extent, but not all the time. I love my parents very much and I don't want them to think this. Please help me.

DONNA, AGE 13, KANSAS

A **It looks to me as though** your parents would have more of a problem on their hands if you didn't talk about boys when you're at home. It's so normal for a girl of your age to be interested in boys that I'd think you were odd if you never brought up the subject. Your father and mother are lucky that your relations with them are so good that you can tell them about what you're thinking and feeling.

Many parents tease their children without realizing their words are being taken seriously. Have you tried joking with them occasionally about boy friends and such? Then, too, remind them that later in your teens you will be devoting a lot of time and attention to college, a career, and so many other things. Right now, getting acquainted with boys on a different basis from that of childhood is in the forefront of your mind.

To be boy crazy really implies a senseless, scattered effort to get attention constantly—in school, at football games, at home, and away from home. Actually, it means tossing aside good judgment and good taste. That's not your case, is it?

Q **In the town where I live,** many of the boys I know and like have cars. My parents won't let me get in a car with a boy driving. Most of my friends can, and I feel left out. I've had many opportunities to go in cars with boys and sometimes I feel like doing it. If I have to wait much longer, I'll lose all my friends. Please give me a definite age when *you* think girls can go in cars with boys.
ANNA, AGE 14, PENNSYLVANIA

A **I think much more depends** upon the *boy* than on his age. Some boys are mature and thoughtful enough to be driving sensibly at sixteen, although at that age they can't possibly have had the wide experience in meeting unforeseen conditions that only long practice can give.

Automobile insurance laws answer pretty conclusively, it seems to me, the question as to why many parents feel hesitant about entrusting their daughters to young drivers.

Parents have to pay higher insurance rates for cars driven by fellows under the age of twenty-five, not just in *some* States, but *all!* But they don't have to pay more insurance for their young daughters who drive. This means that, statistically, riders face greater hazards when boys are at the wheel. Why? They are likely to be more daring, more confident, and to drive faster.

So, let your parents become well-acquainted with the boys you know so that they can judge which ones are brave enough to be careful drivers. Yes, *brave* enough; that's what I mean!

Q My parents are always insisting that I come along somewhere with them, whether it's to a movie, the store to pick up food, or just riding. My brother and sister (seven and twelve) make it a family outing, whatever it is.

The times they are all away are the only chances I get to be perfectly alone, without the everyday noise any family makes. I have to share a room with my sister, so I seldom have my room to myself. They almost always let me stay at home (I love our house) but lately they get mad when I sometimes don't want to go. My father says I *have* to go "because he says so." I don't see the point in always being with the family. Please help me, for it's getting to be a family issue.

TINA, AGE 15, ALABAMA

A **Having some time apart** from their families is necessary for teen-agers, for being alone is one way in which the craving to become an individual, not just a hanger-on to parents, is satisfied. A young person's thinking, dreaming, musing must be done in solitude.

When you do want to stay home, though, it should be for a reason. You might say, good-naturedly, "Oh, if you're all going shopping, this will be a perfect time for me to do my math—alone in peace and quiet—or try a new hairdo."

At other times, you should show your family that you're eager to be with them: "I'd love to go." Occasionally, go with them even if you don't feel like it, and do it without sulking! When they realize that you don't always want to be apart from them, you will meet with less resistance. Do not underestimate the importance of sharing activities. Being a member of a family means doing things together, and is part of what contributes to the warm, secure feeling you cannot find any other way.

Q **I have three problems** in one. My parents don't like my boy friend, and they make it hard for me when he comes over or takes me out. My mother insults him in a joking manner—but she means it. (When she told him he was skinny, I could tell he was hurt.) My father is just as bad. He pretends to forget

my friend's name and calls him every different name under the sun. So far my friend has
laughed it off, but I'm sure he can't take it for
long.

As if this isn't bad enough, my parents constantly criticize me for liking this boy. He's a
clean, decent boy who is very popular at
school. He has friends galore.

I've never seen my parents act like this before. I need help! Thank you.
JUDY, AGE 15, PENNSYLVANIA

A   When you first began to have dates,
your parents knew that your interest in any
one boy was not at all serious. But with each
passing year, parents look more critically at
their children's friends—boys *or* girls—for
there's more possibility of permanent interest.

If this boy is the fine person you believe him
to be, you can brave some of the light, mean-
ingless jokes. But at the first chance you get,
have a talk with your mother and father. You
might ask them to try to remember how they
felt about things like this at fifteen. Explain
that their jokes, aside from ridiculing the boy,

make you feel very uncomfortable. Unless you tell them, they can't know the effect of the words which seem to them to be good-natured fun. Perhaps they have only continued because you do not protest!

Q **Do you think 9:30 P.M.** is too late for a twelve-year-old in the seventh grade to stay up? I've been thinking of asking my parents to make this my bedtime. I now go to bed at 8:30. If it will help you any in answering, I have a six-year-old sister and a ten-year-old brother. LAURIE, AGE 12, NORTH CAROLINA

A **It does help, Laurie,** to know there are other children in your family when considering your bedtime. For if you get permission to stay up later, you can be pretty sure your younger brother and sister will be right behind you, pleading to have *their* bedtimes changed, too. Of course the time you go to bed should fit in with whatever time you have to get up. If you work out a plan that gives you about ten hours sleep a night, you should do all right—unless you tend to need more.

Your parents would probably be more willing to grant a half-hour extension at first than to jump right off to an hour. So start by asking to stay up until 9. Rest easy, Laurie, for as you get older, added school assignments will make it necessary for you to be up later!

Q I feel my parents are very hard on me. If I try to talk to them about their strictness, every single thing I say gets answered, "Watch your language or you'll find yourself up in your room." They tell me what I say is "too sassy," when I am trying to be as nice as I can and don't mean to be sassy at all. I do most of my chores without complaining, and also extra things that I'm not expected to do. And yet I still find them shouting at me. When I've asked to sit down with them and talk about this the only reply is, "We don't need to. Just do as you're told."
LOIS, AGE 11, CONNECTICUT

A Aside from indicating some of the factors that may be involved here, I'm afraid there's little concrete help I can give you. It's often difficult for parents to get used to the idea that their children are growing up mentally and emotionally, sometimes even faster than they are physically, and that the ideas they express are worthy of attention. It's usually much *easier* just to give orders and have them followed than to give explanations of *why* certain behavior is expected.

Another thing—in disciplining their children, parents tend to follow the ways in which *they* were brought up. So the words that are let loose on you are very likely echoes of what your father and mother heard from their elders when they were young. They may not realize this.

I suggest that you say as little as possible when things are heated, so there is no chance that what you say can be interpreted as talking back in a smarty way. Then, at quieter moments, *by all means* continue your efforts to communicate your feelings and thoughts to your parents. Perhaps you would do better if you tried to speak to your mother and father one at a time.

My Mother is My Problem

Q   It seems as though my mother keeps trying to find out everything about me. For
instance, if I'm in my room alone with my girl
friend, she tells us to come out, or says I
should include my seven-year-old brother. So
we have no privacy to talk. I'm scared to tell
my mother my problems because things are
different from when she was young. She
doesn't understand and only gives me a long
lecture. I don't even tell her what goes on in
school. When a boy passes on the street, I
don't dare look at him because she and my
father will make fun of me. They still think
I'm a baby, but I really try not to act like one.
Please help me! ELYNN, AGE 13, NEW YORK

A   If your girl friend is new in the neighborhood so that your mother hasn't had a
chance to form an opinion of her, I think it is
reasonable for her to prefer to be within ear-
shot of your conversations. But if you've
known your friend long enough so that there's

no question about her being a suitable companion, you should have *some* time for the
confidences that are an important part of
young girls' lives. It's just because adults tend
to think teen-agers' talk is "silly" that girls
have to close the door. No one wants to be
heard if poking fun is to be the result!

As for not telling your mother what goes on
at school, I believe you should make an effort
to do so. Surely there are some exciting things
going on or interesting subjects you are studying that you would enjoy sharing with her.
One reason your mother seems to be trying to
learn what you talk about is because she
thinks you are being secretive. And you are
being just that if you don't let her into your
everyday life. The more open and friendly
you are with your mother, the less she will feel
she must insist on sharing the time you want
for private conversation with your friends.

Q I am sure that I am not alone in this
problem, but it does become irritating. The
minute I hang up, after someone has called
me on the phone, my mother starts in with,

"Who was it? What did they want?" and so on. I hate this, but I don't know what to say so she won't get mad. Do you have a solution?
SHARLA, AGE 16, WASHINGTON

A   Yes, Sharla, I have a possible solution, but you may not like it. Why don't *you* start in, before your mother has a chance to, and tell her which friend it was, and what the call was about? If you begin this very open way of handling her curiosity, it may take the edge off it. You needn't give all the details, merely a general impression which will make unnecessary what you consider her "prying" attitude. Of course, you didn't use that word; but it's what anyone is inclined to feel when a great interest is shown in one's affairs—*too* great an interest, you might say.

As an almost-adult person, Sharla, there are beginning to be areas of your thoughts and interests which you prefer not to share fully with your parents. But rest assured that the more you confide in your mother, the more she will trust you.

Q   My problem is my mother! She and the mother of one of my close friends see a lot of each other, and my mom tells her everything about me. She, in turn, tells her daughter "everything." Some of these things I don't want my girl friend to know.

How can I let my mother know, without hurting her feelings, that I don't want her to talk freely about me to Mrs. O. or anyone else outside the family? JANE, AGE 12, ILLINOIS

A   Your mother may be surprised to learn that you cringe at the idea of being a topic of conversation outside your home. Let her know that you were upset to discover that Mrs. O. tells her daughter everything she learns from your mother. Bring up the point that there are things you say to her that you don't wish your girl friend to know. You won't be hurting your mother's feelings, Jane, if you tell her you want to go on talking freely to her, but that you must feel that what you tell her will be held in strict confidence. I think she'll understand.

Q   **My father died** when I was eight years old, and now I am eleven. My mother is planning to marry again; I know who the man is, and I don't like him. When my mother asks me why, all I can say is that he doesn't appeal to me. My mother speaks of how he gives me things, but I like people because they're people, not for what they give me. Mother suggests going to a psychologist to find out what's wrong with me. But I know what's wrong—it's that I couldn't live with him. Mommy and I are growing further apart; we don't do anything together any more. What can I do? CAROL, AGE 11, PENNSYLVANIA

A   **Even if you happened** to like the man your mother plans to marry, Carol, you wouldn't find it easy to share your mother with him. To learn to have less intimacy than you and your mother have been accustomed to for several years is a very big adjustment to make. It is also difficult to accept the idea that your mother puts her husband first, as you undoubtedly will feel many times, whether it's actually so or not.

Have you looked into the future and thought of the long, lonely years for your mother if she does not remarry? You will be with her less and less as your teen-age affairs take up more of your time. What about her when you go away to school or to take a job, and later, when you marry and have a home of your own? Hard as it may seem to set your mind on *learning* to like your prospective step-father, won't that make you happier in the long run than selfishly denying her happiness?

If your feelings persist, you need not fear talking them over with a psychologist. He might help both you and your mother.

Q **I am fourteen,** and want very much to stay for the record hops we have at school. But my mother disapproves of them, says they make too much running around. I don't go on dates, but these hops are different. The teachers are always all there to supervise us. All we do is dance and have refreshments.

Could you tell me if you think Mother is

right? I know she thinks this is for my own good, but *all* the other students go to the hops. PATRICIA, AGE 14, MARYLAND

A   **I'm not quite clear,** Pat, whether it's extra trips to school that are causing your mother's opposition. If the school bus doesn't take you home from the hops, how about trying to arrange to share the driving chore?

Such things as school dances are especially planned to give needed help to students in acquiring social poise and know-how in meeting boys. Being able to get together in a pleasant atmosphere outside of the classroom is important in accomplishing this. We can all be grateful to school heads and teachers who give their time and effort to provide activities such as dances, club meetings, and outings under supervision. In doing so, they are providing important stepping stones in the lives of their students.

Show this answer to your mother and ask if she won't reconsider her rule about not letting you go to the school hops. You might also suggest that she talk to one of your teachers who might be able to give her an idea of how the hops fit into the all-round educational picture.

Q I am an adopted child and I am very thankful that my parents took me. But I have a problem. When a very nice boy asked me for a date, my mother told me she wasn't going to allow me to date until I'm eighteen. As I love being a teenager, I feel that some of the best years of my life will be over by that time. I have tried to talk this over, but I don't get anywhere. I can't even have friends over. One thing I am allowed to do and that is wear lipstick. But what is the sense of trying to make myself look pretty if I'm not allowed to have any fun? MARY, AGE 14, PENNSYLVANIA

A First of all, Mary, you should be aware of two things. Often, adoptive parents are so concerned about doing the right thing for their children that they lean over backward to keep them from making a mistake. At times like this, they are more strict and protective than "own" parents. On the other hand, I have the feeling you might be putting too much emphasis on the fact you are adopted. There are many thousands of "own" parents who are just as strict as adoptive parents, so you see, it's hard to put your finger on the precise reason for their point of view.

As for dating, it is accepted generally that a girl should start dating before she is eighteen, although the exact age depends on her and where she lives. Authoritative books on this subject put forth the idea that dating in the teens is a way of learning to meet new social situations. Schools recognize the need for this learning or training period. That is why they have dances, parties, proms. For the same reason, churches plan picnics and socials to which boys and girls are invited.

Keep up with as many of these group activities as you can, and try to make a social life for yourself even if you do not go out on individual dates. Explain your situation sincerely to the boys you know and continue to be friendly. When the time seems right, ask your mother and father whether you might give a party or invite some boys and girls over after school. As your parents get to know and like your friends, they might very well ease up on their restrictions.

Q **My question is short:** to get an allowance, must you work for it—I mean, must you do chores? This is an important matter to me. PAULA, AGE 10, OHIO

A **My answer, Paula, would have to be** as long as your question is short, if it were to cover fully what is involved in giving allowances! Of course, everyone in a family old enough to do so should have some tasks regularly assigned, as part of his or her contribution to a smooth-running household. But in the opinion of many people who've studied how children learn to use money, chores and allowances should be separate.

Allowances usually take care of one's weekly or monthly needs, like bus fare, lunches, incidentals. Depriving a girl of her allowance because she neglected some duties doesn't do away with her having to have money for daily demands in connection with school. But different families have different ways of handling the allowance business. Many give opportunities for earning extra spending money by parceling out odd jobs around the house that don't fall into a set pattern—like polishing floors, raking leaves, helping to get ready for visitors.

Q   My problem is rather odd. It concerns my younger sister, who is nine and big for her age. My mother is planning to tell her about menstruation. But when she told me about it, several years ago, she merely told me it happened, not how, or why. These things I learned later from the helpful booklets published for girls. The way I puzzled over this makes we wish very much that my mother would help my sister understand fully what it's all about. My younger sister is very curious.

Should I tell my mother how I feel, or do you think she would feel hurt because I would be implying that she didn't tell me very well? JANE, AGE 14, CONNECTICUT

A **I don't believe you need hold** back, Jane, for fear your mother will misinterpret your concern for your sister. The fact that you and she have already talked over the younger girl's need shows you and your mother are open and frank with each other. All you need do, don't you think, is to mention how useful booklets are in bringing about a full explanation?

If you still have any of them on hand you might show them to your mother. She will very likely appreciate your natural and helpful attitude.

Q **My mother has never told me** any of the facts relating to my physical development and its meaning in life. I feel I will never forgive her for that. What I know I got out of a book from the library.

When I asked her about it in the past, she always said she would tell me when she "had time." She never has time to listen to me. I can't talk to her at all. I get self-conscious when I try, so I've just quit trying. Should I

mention it to her, taking the chance she might get angry at me for not trusting her to tell me at "the right time"? Or, should I let it ride until she decides to tell me on her own?
Tina, Age 15, Michigan

A   **It's true, Tina,** that long before the age of fifteen questions come up in every girl's mind that demand explanations appropriate to her age and stage of development.

But what I most want to say, Tina, is to please try to understand your mother instead of being unforgiving. Her silence, which probably amounts to qualms about her ability to deal well with the subject, is shared by a great many mothers who did not have much helpful education along this line when they were growing up. If only they realized that their daughters will more readily accept a hesitant heart-to-heart talk than the forbidding silence that forces the girls to depend on books, or on what they glean from friends!

But a good book often serves as a good bridge between mother and daughter. Perhaps if you were to get again the library book you found useful, and say to your mother, "I wish you'd read parts of this and talk over with me some of the things it says that I don't quite understand," you'd find she'd come halfway across the bridge to meet you.

Q **My question may seem odd,** but here goes. When my mother went to school she did her homework in a completely silent room. Now, when I have homework, and I have plenty in high school, she insists that the room be quiet. As I have from two and a half to three hours of homework, I like to play some quiet music on radio or records, because it makes the time go faster. But my mother says no. It doesn't work to talk to her, I've tried it many times. I'd appreciate your help on a solution. Thank you. JANET, AGE 14, ILLINOIS

A **Quiet background music** helps many people to concentrate and, as you say, it does make the time go more quickly. Nowadays, some of the best scholars study to music, while others must have silence. Some like to sit near a window, while others are bothered by traffic noises. Studying is a personal affair. Whatever works for you is what you should do.

Q **I think I have just about** the most wonderful mother ever, but there is something I don't know how to tell her. Whenever I need something, my mother goes out and buys it; but it never seems to be what I want, and I have no chance to state any preferences. For instance, I had my eye on a purse I wanted, and was hoping to get it when my old one wore out. But without saying a thing, my mother went out and bought me an entirely different one! I keep telling myself, it's the thought behind the gift that counts! But I have more and more shoes, clothes, and so on, that I hate to wear. It's not that I don't appreciate my mother's kindness, but I'm so unhappy about never having any choices. Thank you for any suggestions, for I don't know how to tell my mother about this without hurting her feelings. BARBARA, AGE 15, CALIFORNIA

A **It seems very hard for mothers** to realize that daughters have a way of developing into people with likes and dislikes, ideas, and personal opinions that may not coincide with their own. Any girl should begin to have a voice in the selection of her own clothes from the time she starts school, if not before.

It may help, Barbara, to show your mother pictures of styles you like in magazines and newspapers—before you need a new dress, or purse, or whatever. Mention that you admire this or that, or even definitely say, "I'd love that for fall—or school—or the prom."

When you see something you like in a store, ask your mother to go shopping with you and have a look at it. Too, you might find ways of letting her know you enjoy shopping with her, and ask her to take you along. Point out clothing and accessories in stores, and get her used to the idea that in order to buy wisely for yourself, you must have experience.

Q **All the girls on my street** and in my classes at school wear nail polish. My mother says that I can't have nail polish on. I feel left out, and all the girls tease me. Please understand. Thank you. RUTH, AGE 11, ILLINOIS

A   Somehow I question, Ruth, whether *all* the girls really wear nail polish. I'm sure it seems to you that they do, but I suspect that some of them have only put it on for fun— the way they once clattered around in some of their mothers' high heels—and then found it was too much bother to take off.

I think your mother is right. First of all, many girls your age are still careless about keeping their nails clean. Until a girl sees to it that her manicure is kept up to date, she'd better not embark on polish, which involves frequent extra care. On special occasions it's perfectly fine to wear colorless or pale polish. Once you're in your teens and have learned to take good care of your hair, your skin, and your nails, you'll have shown your mother that you're ready to use polish more regularly. This is not, you see, just a matter of good grooming. It's a question of growing up in many ways.

Q **Since I'm the baby** of the family, I guess my parents never want me to grow up, or at least they act that way. Many of my friends and their parents have asked me to stay over-night, but every time the answer is, "No, we want you at home," or, "You're too young." It's at the point where my friends ask, "Don't your parents ever let you do *anything?*" DIANA, AGE 12, NEW YORK

Q **I'm an only child,** and feel that my mother is over-protecting me. She reads about accidents; so she won't let me learn to swim or skate; and she says the older I get the worse it will be, because I'll want to go in a car with my friends and I might get killed. She wants me to sit home with her. Do you think I'm wrong to want my friends to ask me to join them in sports? I can't talk to her, and I need help. MARLENE, AGE 13, NEW YORK

A **You girls seem to be** up against one of the foibles that afflict some parents—that of hoping to keep children safe by holding them under their eyes. The trouble is, they're *not* safe there! All kinds of serious emotional problems can develop if this cuddling under the family wing endures too long.

You long for and need safe adventure. Learning to live in the outside world comes about through having small bits of independence. Sleeping away from home, with families that your parents know and approve, is one kind of adventure. Learning to swim is another; it is also fun and excellent exercise.

Your parents need help in learning how to let you go. Why not try to get them to discuss with you some ideas that you'll find in books at your local library? "Blueprint for Teenage Living," for example, and others by Dr. William C. Menninger, or "How to Live With Your Teenager" by Dorothy M. Baruch. Parents can get free copies of a Government pamphlet, "The Adolescent in Your Family," by writing to the Children's Bureau, Department of Health, Education and Welfare, Washington 25, D.C.

Q **Like most teen-agers,** I like rock-'n'-roll music. But I have to listen to it on the radio since I haven't any records. My mother doesn't like such music. I don't dare ask her to buy me any records because she wouldn't buy the kind I'd like. *How* can I persuade her to let me enjoy what other teen-agers like? GAIL, AGE 13, WASHINGTON

A   **Perhaps you and** your mother could put your heads together and agree on a selection of records pleasing to both of you. I suspect she fears that if you listen only to "popular" songs, you'll not grow to appreciate classical music. Since top hit tunes fall in favor almost as quickly as they rise to the top, it's best not to invest your all in them. Why not save from your allowance, or earn the money, to buy an occasional favorite record?

Q   **Although my mother lets me** wear stockings, she insists that I wear round elastic garters with them. They are very uncomfortable and are a nuisance since I always have to try to keep them from showing. My mother pays no attention to any suggestions about a garter belt. What can I do? LYNN, AGE 12, ALABAMA

A   Perhaps the best way to approach your mother on this problem, Lynn, is to point out that health factors may be involved. Physicians often say that round garters are inadvisable. If they are tight enough to hold hose snug they may interfere with one's circulation. Garter belts are better because there is no shutting off of circulation. Another solution is one of the various brands of panties with garters attached.

Q   I hope you can help me with my problem. It's about my mother. (I love both my mother and my father very much.) I have many friends at school, but it seems that my mother doesn't like any of them. I'll say, "I'm going out with Sally," to which my mother will say, "Oh, *her?*" Or, when I talk about my friends at home she'll say, "How come you are going around with *that* girl?" I think I should be able to pick my own friends. Sometimes I just dread coming home.
MARIE, AGE 12, NEW YORK

A **I guess you're a victim,** in common with a lot of other girls, Marie, of a belief that's often held by parents that no children are quite so wonderful as their own, and that consequently it takes a great deal of searching to find friends for them who come up to their level.

Remember, the things that appeal to you in the girls you like may not be obvious to your mother, who doesn't know them as intimately as you do. She sees only their appearance—and they may feel awkward in her presence because she doesn't go out of her way to draw them out.

Do tell your mother about the good qualities in your friends and what makes them worth knowing. Ask her, too, just what her objections are—and why?

Q **My mother is forever telling me** how wonderful my girl friend is and how much better she does things than I do. I like my friend very much, but if my mother continues to act this way, I'm afraid I'll hate my friend before long.

I don't think that this is the kind of a problem you can talk over with your mother, for somehow I don't think she will understand. I try to think differently, but I can't help believing that she'd rather have my friend for her daughter than me.

SUSAN, AGE 13, NEW JERSEY

A   **Mothers sometimes expect** an overflow of understanding in their daughters. Of course, deep in your heart you know very well your mother wouldn't trade you for anyone on this globe. But it does get you down to have her sail off into what seems like endless praise of someone else *you* know has faults!

I can't agree with you that you can't talk to your mother about it. She may be surprised, but I think she'll be pleased that you take her into your confidence and tell her how you feel. Ask her in a polite way if she'd like to have your friend as a daughter instead of you. Follow that up by admitting that you get that impression, and are hurt by her comparisons.

As I said before, mothers love their daughters so much that they assume their daughters know this. But sometimes they ride right over those daughters' feelings unthinkingly, as they seem to favor one child over another, or as in your case, wax too enthusiastic over the behavior of someone other than the girl who's nearest and dearest to them.

I Have Difficulty with My Father

Q My problem is that no matter how hard I try to be helpful around the house my father says I'm in the way, or finds something wrong with everything that I'm doing. Even when I cook dinner alone and serve everything as nicely as I can, he tells me I've either put too much gravy in the bowl, or we're missing one serving spoon.

I can't talk to him about it, because the only time he's home is at dinner, and he and Mother are always talking about money or bills. Please help me, for I'm having a miserable time. LOUISE, AGE 13, TEXAS

A   Up with the chin, Louise! I have a feeling that when your father finds fault, he *thinks* he's *teaching* you. I suspect he'd be surprised to learn that you aren't grateful for all the "household hints" he's supplying.

Of course, the dinner table is hardly the place for such lessons, unless they're accompanied with lavish spoonfuls of praise for what you've done right. But remember, it's the end of a long, hard day for him, so try to be patient. Perhaps if you confided to your mother how your father's criticisms make you feel, she could help you open the way for a discussion with him.

Q   My problem is that my father died when I was very little. Now my mother has married again. My stepfather is trying to make me a better person, I know, but somehow he does not seem to do it in a loving way. It seems as if he enjoys seeing me cry. I think I dislike him very much. Would you try to tell me what to do? LOIS, AGE 10, NEW YORK

A **It probably would have been** easier for you to get to love your stepfather if your mother had remarried when you were younger. It is difficult now to share your mother with someone else. Consider, though, that maybe your stepfather finds it difficult, too, to adjust to a young lady who is used to having her mother all to herself.

Is it possible that your stepfather had little contact with children before knowing you, and now is applying some of the ideas he has had about "training" children, which seem to you unduly harsh? (I'm only guessing, of course, since I don't know any details about him.)

Regardless, you seem to understand that he has your good at heart. Knowing this, perhaps during a calm spell you could talk to your mother about the situation and ask her advice about improving it. When your stepfather does anything for you that you can thank him for, be generous with your appreciation. This may "soften" him and help you to reach an understanding. There are so many wonderful things about having a "father" in one's family. It would be a shame if your dislike—which may be only temporary—keeps you from the enjoyment of having a father again.

Q I don't know if my problem is anything new, but it is one I cannot cope with. I love my father very much, and always shall. Lately, however, when he wants to hug or kiss me I won't let him, and I don't know why. It is very obvious that he is beginning to think I don't love him any more, but I do. How can I show him that I love him without hugging and kissing him? LYNN, AGE 14, NEW JERSEY

A Your question, Lynn, is by no means a new one. It's new to *you*, though, because you're entering the period when romantic love and the love for your family begin to split apart. Without quite realizing it you are saving your expressions of affection for the young man you expect to love someday. Of course, you'll keep on loving your father as much as ever, but it will be differently expressed.

You can find many ways of showing your father that you are fond of him. Cater to his comfort! Please him by refraining from arguments about friends, the hours you must keep; show an interest in his conversation; ask him for help on homework—these are just a few of the ways you can reassure him of your deep affection. Why not confide in your mother about your problem? She might drop a hint to your father that you're growing up.

Q **I have a boy friend** who used to call me every night, but since my father didn't approve of this, he now calls me only every two or three nights. Dad still gets angry. He says that my friend probably calls every girl in the neighborhood and I just add to his list. But he isn't that kind of person! Now my father threatens to refuse to let me talk to him at all. I may be sort of young to have a boy friend, but I'm not exactly the prettiest girl there

ever was, and having a boy friend is reassuring. Can you help me? I'd like to keep him.
CONNIE, AGE 14, PENNSYLVANIA

A **Some changes in manners and customs** are easier to get used to than others, Connie. That's all that's the matter. Even a relatively short time ago, when your father was your age, the telephone didn't have the part in the social life of young people that it has today. Now boys and girls have this very convenient way of getting to know each other better than when they're in groups at school or on the way home. A boy who might be too shy to talk to a girl when other people are around can talk in the privacy of his own home without feeling all eyes are upon him.

This doesn't mean I'm standing up for interminable conversations that meander on and on by the half hour while other members of the family who need to use the phone gnaw their nails and tear their hair. What I'm saying is that a five- or ten-minute chat about what went on at school during the day is one of the things families should accept as a way young people get to know each other in a harmless, unthreatening, and inexpensive manner.

Q Long ago, my father gave me the nickname "Cutie Pie." Of course, I am not called that at school, but it's very embarrassing to be called that at home. I don't want to hurt my father's feelings, for he's a very loving father, more so than the average, I'm sure. But how can I make him understand that I'm growing up? DIANE, AGE 10, NEW YORK

A How would it be for you to hunt up some old pictures of yourself, taken when you were five or six years old, and then innocently ask your father if he sees any change in you since those days? For some reason, the grown-up members of a family seem to find it extremely hard to recognize that ten- and eleven-year-olds are *people,* not little children any longer.

Anyone with such a pretty name, Diane, is not expecting too much to want to be called by it. Do tell your father that you are growing up and prefer to be called by your own name.

He will understand. Old habits are hard to break, and he might slip once in a while, but don't be too hard on him.

What Can I Do About My Sister?

Q My problem is that my sister is not very nice to me. She doesn't want me to go any place with her—to football games, movies, or other places. We are fifteen months apart in age, but she still considers me a "child."

My mother has spoken to her about it, but it doesn't help. Please help me solve my problem. BRENDA, AGE 11, RHODE ISLAND

A You may be surprised to hear, Brenda, that there will come a time, not too far distant, when you will be glad you didn't become your sister's shadow. Do you know what sometimes happens when a younger sister "tags along" and tries to become part of an older group? Even when the age difference is slight, she finds that she is missing the close companionship of her own classmates at school. Then, when the older sister reaches the age when dating takes up more of her time and attention, the younger one is really stranded. She feels left high and dry.

Of course I don't for one minute mean that you two should never go places together. But it is very important for you to look for good times with girls and boys who will be with you as you go through school, and on whom you can depend for fun and friendships. Once you do that much on your own, it is very likely that you and your sister will come together on an equal basis—and that there will be times when she'll ask *you* for the pleasure of your company.

Q **My family problem may be an unusual one.** I am fifteen and have two sisters, ten and six. They seem to think that older sisters are made only for taking younger ones out. Like any girl my age, I believe I need some activities that do not include my little sisters. My ten-year-old sister's excuse for wanting to do things with me is that friends her own age don't like her. She blames this on her freckles, but I personally think she's very cute. Please help me explain to her, without hurting her feelings, that I need some privacy when I'm with my friends.

MARIANNE, AGE 15, NEW YORK

A   In some degree, Marianne, your problem exists in every family where there are younger sisters. Little girls tend to want to do everything their older sisters do—from staying up late at night to going to any movie sister and her friends see.

It sounds to me as though you've been unusually patient. Your desire not to hurt the ten-year-old's feelings does you credit, too. But as I see it, this is really your mother's problem. It should be up to her to do the explaining and to be decisive about seeing that the younger girls don't tag along too frequently.

Talk to your mother and tell her that you will plan something every so often with your younger sister and that you and a girl friend will take her along to an occasional movie. When your mother takes over and tells your sisters not to tag along at other times, I think you will find that sisterly fun and personal independence can thrive in the same home.

Q **My sister is fourteen and I am twelve.** We each have our own room. It is like living miles apart, and we are drifting away from each other. It bothers me a great deal to have such a nice sister, with whom I get along so well, and feel this distance between us. We are both very serious and sensitive, which seems to keep me from getting any place when I try to talk it out with her. My parents can't help, for we are old enough to settle it ourselves. But how? Sometimes I feel we are separated because I want to act as mature as she does. What can I do? LORNA, AGE 12, CONNECTICUT

A **For a little while, Lorna,** I'm afraid you must travel paths that diverge. When you were both little girls, your temperaments and likings were apparently close enough to make you more deeply sympathetic and friendly than sisters sometimes are. That has made it all the harder for you to realize that your sister has been outgrowing you in interests, just as she has in physical maturity. For the next two or three years, or even longer, maybe, all the new, exciting activities that come her way will not be shared with you.

So cheer up! This will pass. Try to be interested in some of your sister's activities and tell her about your own doings, but do not expect to share every thought and moment with her. Sisters who have loved each other wholeheartedly, as you have, come together when both reach the adult level. You have a wonderful companionship to look forward to someday.

Q I am twelve, and have two older sisters, fifteen and sixteen. The oldest one is forever borrowing my clothes, and half the time she doesn't even ask. She has as many clothes as I do. What should I do?
CHRISTIE, AGE 12, NEW JERSEY

A Usually, it's the other way round, Christie, with older sisters complaining that younger ones are constantly borrowing their clothes! You might even gently tease your oldest sister about this fact.

Have you tried talking over the situation with her, letting her know how you feel? If that hasn't worked, how about enlisting your other sister's help in a joint campaign to curb Sweet Sixteen's bothersome habit. You might also discuss the whole thing with your mother.

Q **I have an older sister** who is sixteen, very good at sports, and pretty smart. My mother thinks she is wonderful and expects me to be the same way. I try, but I just can't be as good as my sister was when she was twelve, except at swimming—which she doesn't like. How can I show my mother that I'm in any way as good, or as helpful, as my sister?
ANN, AGE 12, MISSOURI

Q **My problem is my brother,** who is five years older than I. He is very cute and has always been popular. Along with this he is exceptionally smart, while I have only a little above average intelligence.

Wherever we go people praise him and pay no attention to me. He has a large crowd of friends, while I have only a few. I tense up when I'm with people who know my brother, for I'm afraid they expect me to be popular the same way. How can I gain friends of my own and get out of the shadow of my brother's popularity? MARILYN, AGE 14, MINNESOTA

A   While some aspects of your problems are different, Ann and Marilyn, you share the uncomfortable position of being over-shadowed by an unusually able and outstand-ing sister or brother. You share something else, too. You both have the sense not to blame the older child in your family; you don't show one bit of the envy that some might feel under the circumstances.

I think you both have traits of character and personality that will make you increas-ingly liked and admired. Go right ahead de-veloping the things you are good at—such as swimming, Ann. As for being helpful, try to do it in your own way, rather than attempting to follow your sister's footsteps. Surely you're not both talented in the same things. Perhaps you can bake scrumptious cookies, although she might be better at shopping for groceries. Your first step is to find your own path and keep on it.

People will admire you too, Marilyn, for your individuality. They don't look for the same qualities in you that they see in your brother. Stop worrying about his abilities and start concentrating on yourself. Go to club meetings, after-school get-togethers, and sports events with girls in your class. Develop interests and friends apart from those in your brother's circle. Both of you should forget about competing and try instead to stand on your own merits.

Q **My little brother, who is two years old,** gets into everything I have while I'm at school. Mother tells me to put things up high on the shelf in my closet, but I can't put *every-thing* on the shelf. When I tell my brother not

to touch, he doesn't pay any attenion. Can you think of a solution?
SALLY, AGE 12, OREGON

Q My sister, who's seven, and I sometimes argue but otherwise are pretty good friends. I have pins I've earned at school and other little treasures. I encourage her to ask my permission before playing with them, but she doesn't listen, and she sometimes breaks or damages them. When I try to tell my mother how I feel, I don't think she understands. I'd appreciate any suggestions.
JANICE, AGE 11, NEW JERSEY

A Although the ages of your younger brother and sister are different, there's much similarity in the questions both of you ask. I'm sure you are generous about sharing many of your possessions with others in your family, but you can't be expected to enjoy having things you care for lost or broken. A two-year-old is itching with curiosity and can't be answerable for touching things if they're where he can get his hands on them. Put as many things as possible out of his reach;

when he is in your room, give him something to play with; try to be patient and continue telling him, "Don't touch," until he is older. This is the best that you can do.

However, the seven-year-old sister is big enough to understand that everyone has some possessions that are valuable to her, and that these should not be used or abused by others. I'm sure your mother would agree if you really explained the situation. Surely she feels the same way about her pet vase or china ashtray.

Why not buy an inexpensive jewelry box for your treasures—many dime stores carry them—and you can take the key to school with you or tuck it out of sight. I think, too, that your sister would enjoy having some trinkets of her own to play with. For her next birthday, how about getting her some dime-store jewelry that will take her mind off your pins?

My Brother is Nice, But . . .

Q   **My problem is my four-year-old** brother. From the little boy next door he has learned some very bad habits, and the language he uses is impossible to describe. As this child is the only one around who is my brother's age, they can't be kept apart.

I am ashamed to bring any of my girl friends home with me after school. Can you help me? I surely hope so.

SANDRA, AGE 12, NEW YORK

A   **I can tell you one thing** that will help, Sandra, and that is for you to ignore the words your little brother repeats at home. The more attention he gets for imitating the boy he plays with, the more he'll persist in the undesirable behavior. He likes the novelty of surprising you and other members of your family, but if you refuse to act shocked by what he brings in, the fun and excitement will be gone for him.

Another thing you can do is read things to him that contain funny words which he'd enjoy adding to his vocabulary. Do you have a copy of Edward Lear's "Book of Nonsense"? If not, get it from the public library, and read aloud some of the very amusing verses and words that Lear invented. (He originally recited these verses to entertain his little friends, as Lewis Carroll did with the ones in "Through the Looking Glass," and children were so amused that the verses *had* to be published.)

In time, your little brother will begin to receive attention for repeating a funny limerick. This—rather than forbidding him to use bad language—is a sound way of helping him to forget his bad habit. And when he's not around, you can explain what you are doing to your friends. Give them a little warning before you invite them home, and tell them not to appear upset at anything your brother might say. They'll be glad to go along, once they know that they are taking part in the cure.

Q **I have a four-year-old brother** who is always asking questions. He thinks I am the very best big sister, and one who knows everything. But he asks many questions that I cannot answer. I want him to have a good impression of me. What should I do?
Janet, Age 9, Minnesota

A **How lucky your little brother is,** Janet, to have a sister who doesn't impatiently turn aside when he appeals to her for information! Especially when one doesn't know the answers to questions, it's a great temptation to brush off the questioner by saying, "Wait until you're older," or "Ask someone else."

Don't worry because you don't know all the answers, Janet. Nobody does! There is more and more knowledge gained every day, month, and year. Even the most intelligent people can't know everything; the really big ones are smart enough to *say* they don't know, but to keep on trying to find out.

There's a tip for you. You can keep your little brother's curiosity alive by helping to answer his questions. If you don't have reference books at home, look up what he asks at the library; or, better still, urge your parents to get a young people's encyclopedia. Only recently, one of our greatest scientists, Dr. Detlef Bronk, said that one of the most pressing needs of our educational system is to keep alive the curiosity that all young children start with, but that gets crushed or stifled if they don't receive encouragement to keep it growing.

Q **Ever since my little brother,** who's seven, was born, I've had to share a room with him. He's untidy, often rude, and I'm sick of sharing my room. I've asked my mother if he can't sleep in my fourteen-year-old brother's room, but she says they don't get along (as if *we* did!). Now that I'm maturing, there are private things I don't want my brother getting into. Please help me! JEAN, AGE 12, TEXAS

Q **I have a very small bedroom,** and my seven-year-old brother sleeps in my room. This is awful because of his junk and toys spread out all over the room. I have no room to do homework. My fifteen-year-old brother's room is tremendous, but when I ask why the seven-year-old can't sleep there, my mother says my older brother needs more privacy. As he is hardly ever there except to sleep, I can't see why he needs all that room. I have friends over—but no privacy whatever.

MARTHA, AGE 12, NEW YORK

A **Your problems are almost identical, girls!** It may be that your mothers are still thinking of their "youngest" as such little boys that they have forgotten for the moment that you've both grown older, and that your needs and interests, so totally different, are even now beginning to clash.

You were probably very devoted to the baby of the family when he was a little pre-schooler. But now that he's a blustering "big boy," who must assert his masculinity, the room arrangement is almost as hard on him as on you.

All things considered, it *is* becoming inap-propriate for a twelve-year-old girl and a seven-year-old boy to room together. It would be preferable if your younger and older brothers could share a room instead. But, you know, the need for a change of this kind sometimes creeps up on parents without their realizing it. Perhaps if you show your mothers this reply to your letters, it will open up the way for discussion.

Q I am 12, and I have three older brothers. I am in the process of physical change, which my brothers tease me about. They toss me comments like, "Here comes our buxom maid," and others I prefer not to write. My mother is not living, and I have no sisters. My embarrassment is made even worse by my father's laughing. Either he or one of my brothers manages to comment when we have company, too. Please tell me why they do this and what to do. MARY, AGE 12, MISSOURI

A It's not only motherless girls, Mary, who are subjected to this kind of teasing. It's a familiar experience to many girls your age who have older brothers.

If I were you, I'd try to laugh along with them when they tease, or turn the tables, teasing back in a kindly way. If you keep cheerful, and pretend to be amused by their digs, they'll ease off. Teasing isn't much fun if the victim doesn't react to the gibes. Isn't it nice to know, though, that your brothers and father realize that you are growing up?

Q **I'm twelve and my brother is thirteen.** He is always saying I'm stupid, and when I accidentally do something wrong, he makes a big thing out of it. I guess I'm at the age when I like my brother, but he seems to hate me. I've tried everything, but nothing works.
VERNA, AGE 12, OHIO

A **Perhaps it hasn't occurred to you,** Verna, that your brother isn't very sure of himself and takes out his feelings of awkwardness and insecurity by criticizing you! When a person feels shaky about whether his looks and actions are appropriate and admirable, he (or she) may try to throw off such feelings by finding fault with other people.

So be patient; don't take his remarks too hard. You can be sure he doesn't really "hate" you; it's just that he has to have a convenient scapegoat for things he's bothered about in himself. His attitude will change in time, but it will require his growing up as much as yours. In the interim, you can help by going out of your way to do nice things for him, being helpful whenever you can, complimenting him even if it is only to notice his latest Scout badge or a new shirt. All boys love this sort of thing even if they growl and pretend they don't.

Q I am fourteen and the oldest child. I have a younger brother and sister, and there's a baby on the way. My mother is very sick and my father works very long hours, so this leaves much responsibility on my shoulders. I must do much of the housework, get meals for my brother and sister, clean up after them, and help them with their homework. I am a sophomore in high school, and have much of my own work to do. I have tried to explain this to my mother and have asked her to make my brother help me. But she says he is a boy and shouldn't do housework. What should I do? DIANA, AGE 14, NEW YORK

A   **If you lived on a farm,** where there were many outside chores to do, there might be good reason for your brother not helping indoors. But living in a city, as you do, there's little excuse for the old traditional division between man's and woman's work. In many situations where parents need help, or when both husband and wife work, it is proper and customary for them and their children (boys and girls) to share the household duties— laundry, shopping, cooking, cleaning, or whatever.

Why not appeal to your father? Tell him you need help and see if he won't set some specific duties for your brother—like vacuuming the rugs on Saturday mornings, putting heavy loads of clothing into the washing machine, carrying the groceries. Or, have you tried sitting down with your brother and having a "man to man" talk with him? Perhaps sharing your feelings, treating him as a complete equal, asking for his advice might work better than anything.

My Problem Is . . .
Friends

Chapter 3

A friend is someone who likes you. It may be a girl or a boy, or a man or a woman. No matter how poised and assured they seem, they have problems, too. They may not be the same ones you have, but they're there. We all hope that our friends will have sympathy for our troubles, tolerance for our shortcomings, and respect for our confidences.

Friendships are more "give" than "take." Be first with a smile and a friendly "hello." If you're a wit, make sure your jibes aren't directed against friends whose feelings may be hurt. Don't offer advice about other people's personal appearance, abilities or social blunders, unless you are asked for it. Rumors and gossip are often without basis in fact. If you pass them along, you may cause untold misery to a friend who is innocent of blame. Discourage this kind of idle chatter or have the courage to stand up for a friend if you know the rumors are not true.

Girls

Q   **I seem to be offensive to the girls** I go around with. Until recently, I was accepted in the group I liked. Now I'm the victim of their criticism and gossip. I'm told it's jealousy, but I'm also called "stuck up." Even my "best" friend doesn't seem to acknowledge me. Can it be possible that I am unaware of a fault that causes everyone's criticism?
PHYLLIS, AGE 13, CALIFORNIA

Q **If no other girl has my problem,** there are a lot of lucky girls! It's that the girls I go around with are really good friends for a couple of weeks, and then poof! Everyone who liked me dislikes me for a couple of weeks. Should I try to find other friends, or just stick to trying to find out *why* they get mad so easily? LINDA, AGE 13, MISSOURI

A **You two have a problem** which is shared by loads of other girls your age. These ups and downs in your friendships are part of the unrest and uncertainties stirred up as girls get ready to leave their childhood behind them.

Each girl is coming to grips with questions that arise within her: "Who am I? Do I have what it takes to make me permanently enjoyable to others? How can I make my favorable qualities outweigh my faults?"

She looks at herself, and wonders about the impression she creates in her friends' minds. And her friends are undergoing much the same experience. During this period a girl often may become as critical of others as she is of herself!

Aside from understanding what causes such capricious behavior, what can you *do* about it? Have a heart-to-heart talk with one of the girls who seems so fickle, to find out if there *is* anything you personally can do about the situation to help remedy it. It's worth a try.

It may be small consolation right now, but your problem *will* diminish as you begin to seek out traits and likings among the girls you know that will correspond with your own emerging interests.

Q **In school every once in a while** I write notes to someone. Then one time someone wrote a nasty note and signed my name to it. Many of my good friends saw it or heard about it, and now no one likes me any more. When I walk up to a group, they stop talking and walk away, and I know they've been talking about me. If you have any information that will help me, I could certainly use it.
MARY, AGE 11, LOUISIANA

A **Your best defense is to act** in such a way that people will begin to realize that you have standards of behavior that you would not dream of lowering. Gossip and rumors have very little chance when your friends know what kind of girl you are. And it will be very hard for them to believe any stories about you that your own actions have proved impossible.

I think, too, you should try not to be so self-conscious and uneasy. The whispering and talking are not flying back and forth as much as you think. The less attention you pay to the gossip, the faster it will die down and be for-gotten.

Q I have a problem and would like your advice on it. I am in a crowd at school. I like all the girls, but when we play together we will not let other people join us. I know how some of the left-out kids feel and I would like to split up our group and play with more kids. How can I do this without hurting my friends' feelings? JANET, AGE 11, MONTANA

A At your age, Janet, it often seems that girls are more concerned with keeping people out of groups than the other way around, so it is refreshing and delightful to hear from you.

It's a part of human nature to want to belong. You are one of a little circle of girls who enjoy and trust one another. But you are independent enough not to need to be clutching the hand of someone on either side of you. Letting go, sometimes, and seeking other companionship, should not make you feel afraid of hurting anyone's feelings. A girl who wants to broaden her friendships and interests, and who is enterprising enough to do so, will be looked up to. Surely you can talk to your group about making new acquaintances; or tell them how nice it would be to get to know some of the girls who've been left out; or explain that occasional breaking up of the group does not mean any less affection or regard between you.

In the long run, your friends will admire you for having a "hands-across-the-sea" outlook, not a next-door-neighbor clinging. Go ahead! Follow your impulse to widen your circle.

Q **There is a very popular group** of girls in our school that just about everyone wishes they could join. My best friend, M., acts so different when we are around this gang. She's a wonderful girl, but when we're with them she acts as if our plans and ideas are ridiculous. For example, we were working on a play both to have fun and to raise money for something special. A couple of days before the play two of these girls asked us what the play was about, and M. said it was just a goofy, stupid play.

Please help me to understand my friend. I like her very much, but if this keeps up, I just don't know.

SHARON, AGE 13, NEW HAMPSHIRE

A **I'm afraid there is** no clear-cut solution to your problem, Sharon, but I can give you some thoughts on how to pave the way.

You say the group of girls is looked up to. This means that somehow, for varied and subtle reasons, the rest of the girls feel "below" the group. It is very human to react to this feeling. Some people, like your friend, act humble and depreciate their own value. Others do the opposite, and are so arrogant and high-and-mighty that they are considered "stuck-up" even though inside they're really as insecure as can be.

Don't be too hard on M.'s seeming treachery to you. When she lets you down, can you laugh and say something like, "Oh, M. is too modest to admit that we're a pretty sharp pair when it comes to using our brains." At other times, you ought to speak up and give your own opinion. You can say very pleasantly, for instance, "Oh, do you think so, M? I thought the scene we worked on yesterday was so funny . . . I'm sure everyone will love it." Going even another step, you might find a moment when the two of you are talking quietly to gently ask about the difference in her attitude when you are with others. Certainly, you can help this girl you're fond of to strengthen her belief in herself and her ability to meet others on their own ground.

Q **My best friend is so quiet** when we are with the rest of the girls that it is costing both of us our popularity. Many of the girls have told me they don't like her. But she's my best friend and I'm concerned about her. When I ask her why she's so quiet, she says she can't think of anything to say. It usually ends in our staying by ourselves. I get along with the other girls when I am with them, which isn't often.

I don't know whether it was right for me to tell my friend what the others said. It hasn't had any results, but I thought I was doing the right thing. I'd be so grateful for any help with this disturbing problem.
PATRICIA, AGE 13, CALIFORNIA

A **You are a wonderful friend,** Pat, for sticking to the Quiet One. But it would be a mistake to be *too* self-sacrificing. There are many good reasons for spreading your companionship among a number of girls and learning to get along with many different personalities. Don't drop the Quiet One, but do switch to more frequent contacts with the other girls, and try to widen your circle of friends.

You were right to tell your shy friend about how the other girls feel. If you're willing, you can do even more to help her. Since you spend so much time together, she obviously talks to you. Use some of the things she says to draw her out in a group. Try to bring her into the conversation in small ways: "That book Sheila read about exercising is good . . . what was that part about legs, Sheila?" You can even tell your friend that you're going to try small prompting tricks to help her—so that in the end both of you will have more fun.

Q **When our crowd started** high school last fall, a new girl began to be very popular, and it wasn't long before she was class treasurer and cheerleader. I liked her at first, but later began to resent what she "got away with," like going to a party she wasn't invited to. One day at the lunch table she began to ask who of those she'd invited to a slumber party were coming for sure. She went down the row saying, "You're coming? You're coming?" until she got to me, then skipped me, and continued. It made me feel bitter. All winter she had been friendly, but I have a nice sliding hill where all the kids like to come. Nobody stays mad at her, but I want to have a feeling that my friends are faithful, and now she never asks me to join in anything. Would it be right if I had some kind of party and did not ask her? DIANA, AGE 14, OHIO

A   Too bad, Diana, that there are people like that. It's little short of infuriating to see people riding roughshod over others, accepting favors from them, and then coolly ignoring them. To speak to the other girls about her slumber party in your presence was rude, a snub that may have been only thoughtless, but could have been intentional.

Such people as this girl serve a very useful purpose, though that's not the light we see them in when we're personally black-and-blue from being bumped into by them! They show how *not* to behave if we want to have friends who cherish and trust us. Now you can decide about inviting her to your party on this basis: ask yourself, "Would I be leaving her out just to 'get back' at her?" If that turns out to be so, you couldn't feel very comfortable, could you? Being generous and forgiving never disappoints, in the long run. So invite her if you enjoy her company and if you're sure the others you ask will, too.

Q **One of my good friends** is forever criticizing me. I don't think it's "constructive" because it often hurts my feelings. (Plain, helpful criticism doesn't bother me badly.) She also repeats things other girls have said about me.

Recently I fixed my hair in a new, flattering style, but she immediately tried to brush it another way. I don't think she's jealous of me, unless she's sensitive about not having as good a figure as I happen to have. She tells me everything she thinks is wrong with me daily —my eyes, clothes, and all, and laughs at what she says is my "sentimentality."

She's intelligent and often lots of fun, but I don't want her to run over me. I'd hate to criticize her back, for she's emotional about it, and it would seem so cruel.

JOY, AGE 13, GEORGIA

A **Apparently, Joy,** you value this girl's friendship enough so that her censure isn't causing more than surface scratches so far. But before these "scratches" become infected with bitterness or the venom of vanity, let her know that you don't like her carping. You can call a halt to her use of you as a whipping post without lashing out in return.

Have you ever actually asked her why she persists in criticizing you? Possibly if you knew why, you would find it easier to ignore. Often, finding fault with others is a telltale sign of dissatisfaction with oneself. We notice and are irritated by qualities in other people that we may or may not suspect are our own imperfections. Next time she begins, muster your sense of humor and stop her by lightly reminding her that compliments are in vogue nowadays, too.

Q   **For many years** I've been friends with a wonderful girl. Lately she's been asking me to lend her money, saying, "I'll pay it back tomorrow." So far, she has never paid me back, but keeps asking for more. All told, the amount she has borrowed is small—should I ask her for it? My mother thinks it would be impolite, but we are both puzzled as to what to do. SUSAN, AGE 13, WISCONSIN

A   **You're not really doing** your friend a favor, Sue, by lending her money she doesn't return. Whatever her reasons may be for borrowing, the amount should be repaid—and as promptly as possible. If you are really a good friend, you will help her to overcome this poor habit.

The next time she asks to borrow, you might say, very kindly, "I really can't lend you any more because you haven't paid back what you've already borrowed." Or you might ask her politely if she's forgotten what she owes you—that you thought of it because "I need some extra change for my lunch today." If she tells you how forgetful she is about such things, you might suggest that she write herself a little reminder note from now on. In the end, you will be doing her a far greater service than the one to yourself.

Q **My problem is really troubling**—and I hope you can help. While I was in grade school everything seemed perfect—my grades, friends, everything! But now that I'm in junior high I am confused, for I have never met a group like my classmates. I know there are a lot of different kinds of people in the world. But I don't think there are over four girls in my room who don't swear and are not dirty-minded. My friends who live around me are very nice, and they will not understand if I run around at school with such kids. But who will I be with at school if I don't, for my real friends are in different rooms and classes and have different lunch hours?
NANCY, AGE 13, MISSOURI

A **If there is no way** you can see more of your neighborhood friends at school, I think you would be justified in asking your mother to help. If she will talk over your problem with your teacher or counselor, or even the school principal, he may arrange to separate you from your present class.

Some of these girls whose behavior you disapprove of may not have had the fine home standards you have enjoyed, so be careful not to have a "holier than thou" attitude which they might think was snobbishness. If you manage to change classrooms you could explain that it's in order to be with a group from your own immediate neighborhood.

Q There is a girl in our crowd whom we all like, but who doesn't use a deodorant. This is becoming very offensive, and we are afraid she'll lose all her friends. Should we tell her, and if so, how can we do it without offending her? She's a very nice, sweet girl except for this. Thank you for considering our problem. MARY AND HELEN, AGE 15, GEORGIA

A   This is a delicate problem and, as you suggest, needs to be handled tactfully. Perhaps when the three of you are together, you might bring up the subject of good grooming, discussing various bits of advice that had been most helpful to you and mentioning casually that beauty experts agree that during the teen years (when glands are active and whenever nervousness causes excessive perspiration), it is especially necessary to use a deodorant, ending with mention of the one you prefer. Or, failing this, you might ask the school nurse to talk to your friend about the problem.

Q **I have never had a bedroom of my own,** because of our cramped quarters. My parents let me accept invitations to stay overnight with my good friends, but I hesitate to accept, because I can't ask them back. I don't have any sisters, just brothers, so there's no way of doubling up. Should I say "no" when girls ask me over? SUSAN, AGE 12, CALIFORNIA

A **By all means, Susan,** accept those invitations from your good friends. You can reciprocate in whatever ways you are able to. How about asking permission to have them over for dinner or plan a party and invite them? Your friends will probably understand without your having to say a word in explanation.

And perhaps, as time goes on, your brothers will go on overnight hikes, or to camp—or even be staying overnight with *their* friends. In any such event, you might ask permission to use their room.

Boys

Q My problem is one lots of girls must have. It is small, but one I can't seem to overcome. When a boy asks me out, I refuse because I don't know how to act. I don't know what to do or say, though I've been on a few dates. So now, when I'm asked, I say no. I hope more than ever that you can help me. MARY, AGE 15, NEW YORK

A I'm sure you realize, Mary, that turning your back on a problem never solves it. Perhaps you can build up courage by looking at the problem from the boy's angle. To bravely say "yes" the next time a boy asks you for a date would save him from the humiliation of being turned down. Remember, a boy has to pluck up *his* courage to invite a girl out, and he always faces the possibility of a "no." When you refuse, how can he help but wonder what's wrong with him?

Behavior on dates also involves a two-way responsibility. A boy has qualms about whether he's doing the right thing, so it's up to the girl to try to make things pleasant and easy. For instance, if he asks which you'd like, ice cream or a soda, don't say, "I don't care." State your preference! Help him out, too, by being enthusiastic about anything he suggests. "I *love* to roller-skate," or "I've been dying to see that movie!"

For first-rate advice, read "Smarter and Smoother," by Maureen Daly (Dodd, Mead & Co.). A book that includes tips on gentlemanly behavior, as well as that of ladies, is "This Way, Please," by Eleanor Boykin (Macmillan).

Q   My problem is one that concerns dating. Several times a boy called me and asked me to go to a party with him. Though I like him very much, I refused because it seemed a little late. Should you accept a date even though there is a possibility someone else was asked before you? ANNA, AGE 13, RHODE ISLAND

A   Your friend's last-minute invitations may be due to timidity, rather than to your being second choice. Sometimes a boy puts off calling a girl because he's afraid he'll be turned down—with the result that he *is* snubbed for waiting too long. Boys are as sensitive about making overtures along social lines as girls are, so give them the benefit of the doubt and cheerfully accept. Too, if you really enjoy this boy's companionship, why not accept—even if you are second choice? The decision really boils down to this: going out and having fun or staying home alone with your pride.

Q   We moved here six months ago, and for three months I've been dating a boy I met at school. We've had a lot of fun together, but then out of a clear blue sky he just ignored me at school for about a week. He has been tak-ing different girls to basketball games, and it really hurts to see him with them.

Last week we had a dance to which girls had to ask boys, and I invited him. He acted as though he had a very good time, but since then he's just said hello to me at school and ignored me at lunchtime. If I went out with other boys, he would probably get the impression that I don't like him and never ask me out again. I like him so much I don't want this to happen. Please help me.

DONNA, AGE 16, KANSAS

A Actually, Donna, three months was quite a long time for either of you to remain interested in each other to the exclusion of others. You know it's normal for teen-age relationships to be brief, to change and shift. Most boys don't like to have the impression prevail that they are the sole property of any one girl. And in a little while, you yourself might have found your interest in this boy waning.

You don't mean to say you're really thinking of hanging around forlornly rather than dating other boys? You don't need to pretend rapturous interest in everyone you go out with. But you should certainly try to have a good time and forget worrying about your former beau.

By all means, take his lessening interest in your stride and for what it is—a natural and healthy reaction. If, incidentally, he happened to renew his interest in you, he would do it whether you went out with other boys or not.

Q **For about four months** I went steady with a boy before breaking up with him. Since I told him I didn't want to go with him, he has been spreading untrue rumors about me. It hasn't spoiled my popularity, and I have many friends. But now when boys take me out, they seem to think they can get something out of me, from what this boy has said. Please help me. JUDY, AGE 14, CALIFORNIA

A **Only boys who are insecure** need to brag and boast to other boys about their conquests among girls, Judy. One of the reasons you broke off with him may have been that you found he was not manly, in the best sense, so your intuition told you that you'd be better off not becoming too dependent on him as a boy friend.

I don't wonder you feel at a loss to make sure your reputation doesn't suffer from his remarks. But don't worry; if you are fun to be with, but dignified and restrained enough so that the boys you date realize you have no intention of letting them go too far, they'll soon recognize that the rumors were false.

You may feel, as time goes on, that you've learned something from this experience, unpleasant as it was. And I think you'll find that the boys you like the most are those who have *many* interests, and are so busy with activities and sports that they don't have too much time or inclination to set themselves up by spreading tales.

Q **The boy I like is a little younger** than I am. Some of my girl friends think it is proper for me to like him as long as we both like each other. The other part of my problem is that though he has told me he likes me, he acts coldly when we are with other people. Should I just forget him? FRANI, AGE 16, MARYLAND

A **There must be ways** in which your friend is quite as mature as you are, Frani, or you probably wouldn't enjoy his company. Each individual has differences in personality that set him apart from others far more than a difference in age does. So forget that he's younger; this will be the best way of keeping him from being self-conscious about it.

Many a boy has such a dislike of being thought sentimental that he steers away from showing any glimmer of his feelings in public. The more at ease you act in your friend's company, the easier you make it for him to be natural, too.

Q **For six years** I attended a parochial school. Although it was co-ed, the boys and girls did not mingle in classes. Now I've transferred to a public high school, and I'm having trouble adjusting to having boys in my classes. Despite my being a new girl, a boy I admire asked me to an important school dance. I'm terribly afraid to go because I don't know how to act around boys.

Another thing that worries me is that I hope to become a doctor. Not knowing how to act with boys would be a sorry setback. I'd be grateful for any advice you can give.
<small>ROSEMARY, AGE 15, NEW YORK</small>

A **A girl as foresighted** as you show yourself to be, Rosemary, should have her problem well out of the way in short order. You are quite right. Learning to adjust to boys now will help later in medical school where boys always outnumber girls.

But you must be doing pretty well to have been sought out as a date for an important event. Obviously, boys do not feel ill at ease in your presence. It is up to you to push yourself into speaking up in co-ed classes, into smiling and being friendly, even if it seems forced at first. But every little achievement will make the next easier, and your fears will wear away gradually.

As for learning how to behave on dates, re-read back issues of THE AMERICAN GIRL Magazine that contain practical articles on this subject; and check your public library for a popular book on dating, such as "The Art of Dating," by Evelyn M. Duvall.

Q **I go to dances,** but I never dance, though I am fairly cute and have a pleasing personality. Before I moved here from the North, I was very popular with the boys. Now, they dance with other girls, but never with me. I always try to look neat and well-dressed. Please help me, for I am very unhappy and mixed up.
CAROL, AGE 13, TENNESSEE

A **Has it occurred to you,** Carol, that you might have to change your personality a bit to fit in with the slightly different manners and customs of the South? Perhaps your habits of talking and acting vary in subtle ways from what the boys are used to. If so, they may feel uneasy and shy away from you until a trial period has made you seem less unusual. It could be, too, that you've shown you miss the companionship of long-time friends. Or, without being aware of it, you may have compared your new surroundings unfavorably with your old home town and friends. This sort of thing —however mild—would not be happily received, and you'll have to watch your words very carefully during these first months.

Be on the lookout for local conventions and try not to behave contrary to them. Patterns of social behavior differ considerably in various sections of the country; a person who is truly cosmopolitan can adapt gracefully anywhere.

Q **My problem is that** I am not allowed to go out with boys until I'm sixteen. I am well-liked by boys and girls, and I'd like to know what I should tell a boy when he asks me for a date. I've been up against this problem and didn't handle it very well, for I hurt the boy's feelings. I hope you can help me.

KATHY, AGE 14, MICHIGAN

A   **Under the circumstances** you outline, Kathy, I think absolute honesty and frankness are the very best policy in turning down a date without hurting a boy's feelings. If you come right out and say you haven't any choice in the matter, that your parents believe that sixteen is young enough for you to begin dating, I fail to see how a boy could take it amiss. How about adding, "I'm sorry, but you see how it is."

Q   **Recently I went to the movies** with a girl friend. Toward the middle of the movie a nice-looking boy asked me if I would sit with him. I said "No," because I am not in the habit of sitting with boys I don't know. I don't neck, and he didn't look like the type, either. Did I do the right thing? He was dressed neatly and looked very nice, and now I think maybe I should have sat with him and gotten to know him. I'm sure other girls have this same problem. MARIE, AGE 13, CONNECTICUT

A **You did exactly the right thing,** Marie. The very fact that he asked you to sit with him tells you something about him that *isn't* quite so nice! A boy who tries to pick up a girl isn't gentlemanly. If, for instance, he had been sitting among a group of schoolboys you knew so that they could have introduced him to you, the picture would have been entirely different.

To be fair to this boy, he may not have known any better. It's surprising how many parents forget to provide the basics of good social behavior. Well, this kind of information cannot be picked out of the air we breathe. But everyone *can* find help on the public library shelves. "Manners for Moderns" is a stand-by book by Judith Scott for both boys and girls; while if you want to befriend some boy of your acquaintance, you'll tell him about "He-manners," by Robert Loeb.

Q **I usually sit down and** try to reason out my own problems, but this one has me baffled. The other day I was waiting for the light to change, when a convertible stopped right in front of me. One of the boys in it turned around, smiled, and said, "Hello." I turned my head the other way. Was I being snobbish?

A similar thing happened when I was riding my bike one day on my way to my girl friend's. I stopped a minute to fix my sweater when three boys coming from behind called out, "Turn around. We want to see what you look like." I was scared and didn't know what to do, so I quickly rode off. Was this the right thing to do? MARGARET, AGE 14, MICHIGAN

A **You were neither** snobbish nor rude, Margaret. The rudeness was on the part of the boys who spoke to you. A girl who wants to be a credit to her upbringing is wise not to smile or speak to boys who are strangers to her, no matter how much their whistles or remarks *seem* to flatter her. You did the ladylike thing to ignore them. (I hope you don't think I am being old-fashioned to favor "lady-like" behavior; there's really no other word that describes quite so well the modesty and dignity that become a girl.)

Q **I go bicycle riding** quite often and sometimes see boys with whom I go to school. But I never know whether the boy or girl should speak first. I am afraid if I ignore them until they speak, they will think I am stuck up, when I'm not, really. MICHELE, AGE 12, TEXAS

A **When boy and girl acquaintances meet,** no matter where, it's up to the girl to speak first. Often, a girl needn't do more than smile before the boy begins to acknowledge their knowing one another. It is ladylike to show your willingness to be greeted with a cordial word or look. You are absolutely right in thinking you might be accused of being snobbish or boorish if you failed to do so.

Q **This isn't just our problem,** but that of all the girls in our group. The boys we know are mostly fourteen, as we are, but sometimes they don't act their age. We girls are past the kissing-game stage, and we'd like to have some regular party-type fun at parties. But the only kind of party the boys consider good is one at which they can play kissing games. Don't get us wrong! Outside of parties, when we go together to parades, football games, and movies you wouldn't know these boys carried such ideas in their heads. It's just at parties that they get carried away. Must we just sit patiently, or is there something we can do to change their attitude?

GINNY AND JOYCE, AGE 14, NEW YORK

A   Girls are about a year more mature than boys at your age, and this often puts an obstacle in the way of easy socializing. This difference in development shows up even earlier, when boys are reluctant to dance at a time girls are eager to.

You're lucky in having so many things aside from parties that you can enjoy together. Why not try encouraging more after-the-game snacks in the kitchen and depend on school dances, social affairs at church, and other well-supervised social doings. That way there will be fewer opportunities for kissing games and more for the wholesome fun you mention. If you do have a party, plan to keep things moving with a variety of interesting games. And never underestimate the power of tempting refreshments to distract the boys if they start getting "carried away."

Q **My problem may be common,** but it has me thoroughly confused. I won't let boys kiss me. Of course I wouldn't let just *anyone* kiss me, but when I'm with a boy I really like, I don't object to his holding my hand or putting his arm around me. If he tries to kiss me, though, I freeze up and draw away. Can you help me? I'm very upset about this.
MARY LOU, AGE 15, INDIANA

A **Your feeling is more common** than you realize, Mary Lou. A great many girls shrink from intimate endearments, and naturally so. It is just the human self-protective instinct coming to the fore, telling you to wait awhile. Your reaction shows that either you have not known a boy long enough to feel completely at ease or what you consider liking has not yet developed into real fondness and affection. You can rest assured that a few years from now, when the right boy comes along and you feel "Our friendship has a real meaning, and we are truly fond of each other," you will react differently to a kiss. Up to that time, don't let yourself be swayed into allowing familiarities that make you uncomfortable. You can make sure (if you want to) that a boy understands by telling him frankly that you aren't singling him out for this cool treatment.

Q How do you ask a boy for a date? I've just messed up my first attempt. I was supposed to ask a boy to a dance and decided to invite a good friend of mine who's a year ahead of me in school. I was awfully scared about calling him, but finally did. I started out just fine. I asked him if he had a date for the night of the party. When he said he did, I was so startled I said, real fast, "I guess I'll have to call someone else," and hung up. I'm sure he'll never speak to me again! Please help me. MARILYN, AGE 12, TEXAS

A   **Cheer up, Marilyn, none of us is** born "poise perfect." This situation may have taught you something very useful about giving an invitation to either a boy or a girl. Put yourself at the other end of the line. Being pounced on with a question at the outset of a conversation puts you at a disadvantage. You may not know at that point whether you want to accept. Even if this boy hadn't had a date for the night of your party, he may not have wanted to commit himself before knowing more details. You might have begun along these lines: "Our club is having a dance on such and such a date, and I hope you can go with me." Then, suppose he's a boy who hasn't yet any interest in dancing, he can say, "I'm sorry, but I'm going to be busy that night," without hurting your feelings or exposing his shyness about dancing.

So, by giving an explanation at the start of your call, you won't take the listener by surprise and you will give him a chance to organize his thoughts—*and* his feelings.

Also, instead of feeling embarrassed, and dropping the matter, the very next time you saw this boy you might have said, "I was sorry you had a date for that night and couldn't come to the party," thus letting him know you didn't mean to be abrupt.

Q **This is my first year in high school,** and I haven't gotten to know many boys yet. It seems that at all the dances I have the same problem. A boy comes up and asks me to dance. If I accept, he asks me again. I'm not the type of girl who goes with "just anyone," and when some boy I don't particularly like keeps asking me to dance all evening, I don't know what to do. I don't have the heart to say "No." What can I say instead? I don't want to seem stuck-up or anti-social. Is this a common problem?
Rosanne, Age 14, New Jersey

A **It's a great deal commoner,** Rosanne, for girls to complain of being wallflowers!

There's an easy solution to your problem. Simply look around for a girl who's not dancing, then take the boy over, make any necessary introductions, and begin talking with her. After taking pains to say you've enjoyed dancing with him, you may excuse yourself and move away. But be sure to accept graciously if he asks you to dance again later on.

Naturally, you'll have to take the risk of being partner-less for a spell. But this way, the others will not get the impression that you are "his" girl, even for the evening.

My Problem Is . . .
School

Chapter 4

You hear on all sides today how difficult it is in our automated, complex, modern society to have that full rich life we all desire without more and more education. So for that successful adult life you dream about, get as much education as you possibly can. Take advantage of the opportunities these school years offer for study, for forming friendships, and for gaining a greater understanding of yourself and others. As early as you can, plan your curriculum with your adviser, so as to meet the requirements for whatever you wish to do after high school.

Don't miss out on the hobbies and extracurricular activities that are fun and often point the way to a career. Do your own work—copying from others is only cheating yourself—and do not permit others to cheat themselves by copying from you. Make the most of your years in school to build a satisfactory life for yourself.

Q   The girl who sits behind me in school is always copying my work, asking questions during tests, and wanting me to do her homework. I make an A average in school, and happen to do my best in subjects she hates. I have told her "No" lots of times, and then she gets me into trouble by saying I was talking in school. Our teacher says next time we are both going to get into serious trouble. He won't allow either of us to change our seats.
ELIZABETH, AGE 11, OHIO

A   This kind of trouble, Elizabeth, should be handled by your teacher. But if he is as unaware as he appears to be of what's going on, it's time for you to ask your parents for

help. Ordinarily, complaining at home of un-
fairness at school is a very dubious way of
handling one's problems. But in this case it
seems justified. Or, you might explain your
situation to your school adviser—if you have
one—who would be likely to come up with
a course of action. You can't continue making good grades if you're constantly distracted
in this way.

Q   During an exam, I saw a boy take his
notes out of his desk for help with the answers.
Apparently no one else saw him do it. When
the results of the test came out, he had the
highest mark in the class. Should I tell the
teacher? This has been bothering me.
LINDA, AGE 12, RHODE ISLAND

A   To be considered a tattletale is far from
desirable, but so is cheating! Because the one
really hurt is the boy himself, it is not up to
you to do anything. If his cheating had
harmed another student, that would be another matter. What you can do is to ask your
teacher to hold a discussion about cheating

in which class members state their feelings about "telling on" those who take unfair advantage. Perhaps you can form some kind of honor system. In any case, the subject should be discussed openly.

No one really gets very far by cheating in exams. The slightly higher mark a person gets is more than offset by the damage to one's self-respect. Sneaky behavior and dishonesty leave a mark—inside if not outside. Although this boy might have fooled the teacher this time, she will catch on soon if his classroom work and his test papers don't jibe. The same applies to the girl who copies her friend's homework papers. Sooner or later, the teacher recognizes the similarity and figures out what's going on. A really smart girl knows better than to hand in work done by another, for she knows the time will come when she'll *have* to stand on her own.

Q   **A girl who sits next to me at school** is always asking to see my papers. I don't mind letting her see my work, but she often uses my answers on her papers. She is a good friend of mine, and I want to know how I can discourage her doing this without making her angry at me. SUE, AGE 11, MASSACHUSETTS

A   How can you say she's a good friend, Sue, when she's robbing you? That's what it amounts to, isn't it? For her own sake, as well as yours, you must put a stop to her practice of cheating. By letting her take your answers, you are aiding her in the deception she seems to be getting away with.

If she is really a girl whose friendship is of value, chances are the relationship will survive your refusal to hand over your work. Her "hurt" will actually be anger at herself, for she'll feel guilty. I think that if you refuse tactfully, she'll be grateful in the end.

Q   When I came to this new school this year I made up my mind I was going to like science, which I've not been too good in. But my teacher in that subject turned out to be awful. He acts as if he were commanding an army. There are some people you just can't like, and he is one of them.

As a result, I'm beginning to do poorly in his class. Last year I had almost an "A" average, and I don't want my marks to go down. Please help, for I'm at the end of my rope! FRANCES, AGE 12, NEW JERSEY

A   **There are bound** to be occasional clashes of temperament between teachers and their students. When you stop to count the number of teachers you will have through the years, it would seem phenomenal if you were to like all of them.

If you make up your mind to it, your strong feeling can spur you to do *better* work in this class. So it's like being in an army? Why not play the part of a good soldier then and discipline yourself to take orders? Soldiers don't always like what they do, but they respect the reason for it. You are going to be under the command of your teacher for only a short time. You don't have to like him, but perhaps you can respect him—for his vast scholarship, for his years of training, for his dedication to science and to teaching. You can also work and study hard on your own because you respect your goal—that of gaining knowledge.

Learning self-discipline is one of the big features of growing up. When you come up against an obstacle you can't climb over, accept it and make the best of it. Never let it get the best of you.

Q My problem has been bothering me since I was in fifth grade, and as I'm now in seventh, you can see it's a long-lasting one that doesn't get any better.

I was good enough in school so that I got all "A's" until in fifth grade another girl began to do as well as I, or better. Soon she was teacher's pet. The teacher told me I was stupid and I began to think so myself. Ever since then, when anyone criticizes me or gets angry with me, I feel as though they are telling me that I am too dumb to be associating with them.

Please tell me how to handle this serious matter. JUDY, AGE 12, KANSAS

A   Perhaps it's just as well, Judy, that you found another girl rivaling you early in the grades. For that's bound to happen sooner or later. And if a person has been tops in her class until she gets to high school or college, this is a much harder jolt than the one that has jarred you.

Let me say at once that it is possible you could have misunderstood the teacher who used the word "stupid." Even if she implied it, it was a breach of good taste, to say the least. But whatever the case, you mustn't let it grow into a giant monster, all out of proportion. Have you let a few words keep you from applying your best efforts to your work? Have you let your hurt over having a competitor throw such a shadow that you are no longer living up to what you *can* do? Surely you have more bounce than that!

Don't make the mistake of imagining your friends consider you "dumb"; for that's all it is—imagination. We all must learn to laugh off small slights and even ridicule at times. When you are tempted to belittle yourself, just try to imagine that you are another girl looking at Judy from arm's length. There. Isn't that better? Don't you agree it's just a matter of getting a little perspective?

Q I have something on my mind, and here it is. I admire one of my teachers very much. Some of the kids don't think her face is pretty, but they say beauty is in the eyes of the beholder, and in my eyes she has a beautiful face and figure. I'd like to tell her how I feel. Should I tell her or not? And if yes, how should I tell her?
Yvonne, Age 13, New Hampshire

A You've already told her, Yvonne. Your admiring eyes and your respectful behavior in class have told her far better than any words how you feel. It would only embarrass her to have you try to express your admiration. If you wish, you might mention that you like a particular dress or hairdo, but don't overdo it. The good work you do and the interest you show in your studies will be the very best ways to reward and compliment your teacher.

Q   As an eighth-grader, I have homework almost every night. When I run into trouble, I *try* to ask my parents, but all they say is, "Do it yourself." Then, if I can't do it, I have to let it go and get poor grades in school. What can I do to make them see that I need help?
BARBARA, AGE 13, MONTANA

A   Could it be, Barbara, that the subjects with which you most often have trouble are ones that your parents are not too familiar with? You could hardly expect them to know much about the new methods of teaching math.

Or perhaps it's that your parents honestly believe that homework is something you're supposed to do without help. Either way, when homework problems have you really stumped, why not enlist your teacher's aid? After all, her chief concern is that you learn and understand what she is teaching. If you explain to her the difficulty you're having, she would probably be more than willing to spend a little extra time with you to help you straighten out your problem subjects.

Also, a note from your teacher or a discussion at a parent-teacher meeting about the importance of your parents' interest in your school work would make them more aware of how you feel.

Q   **This is a very hard problem** to solve by myself. I am fourteen years old. Somehow, when I was in the seventh grade I got into the wrong group, that was always getting into trouble. We didn't do anything bad, but they are a sort of low kind of kids that I don't want to go with. I'm now in the ninth grade, and in school I am put in the same group that I went with earlier. My best friend is not in this group, and I have been trying to get into classes with her, but they won't let me change. I have been trying so hard not to associate with the wrong group. What should I do?
MARILYN, AGE 14, CALIFORNIA

A   Of course I don't know how they group students in your school, Marilyn, but it may be that a difference in your grades, your rating on achievement tests, or some other technicality, is responsible for your difficulty in getting assigned to classes with your friend. I believe, though, that it would be well worth while to go to your school counselor and tell her very frankly why you want to make a change. While it may not be possible for her to assign you to new classes, she may be able to advise you about activities that would bring you in contact with a variety of students.

Surely you can do a lot on your own. You can be polite to your old friends, but you needn't continue to join them, say, for after-school snacks, or to be close in any other way. Join clubs that are open to all, offer to help whenever volunteers are called for, and continue to show by your behavior that you are a thoroughly nice girl who has high standards. Don't depend entirely on school associates for social life, but take an active part in functions that are planned for and by

young people at your church or in other outside groups.

My Problem Is . . .
A Career

Chapter 5

Lucky you if you are sure at an early age just what you wish to be and to do with your life, and can plan your studies accordingly. Most young people are uncertain. There are many things you can do now, though, which may help you later to make that big decision the right one.

Almost all high schools today, and many junior high schools, have assemblies at which specialists address students who would like to explore career possibilities in a particular area. Plan to attend as many of these sessions as you can. Try out hobbies and extracurricular activities that interest you and may possibly point the way to a career. As you move into the older teens, you may have opportunities to sample careers that appeal to you through part-time or summer jobs. Nobody thinks you will decide firmly to be a doctor, or a lawyer, or a plumber, or an atomic physicist until you have had an opportunity to know more about yourself and your aptitudes and abilities, and more about various career possibilities, but you may be helped to decide what kind of high school or college training you want.

Q **I'll give my problem a try,** though it may sound queer. As long as I can remember, I've wanted to be a service nurse and would especially like to be an Air Force nurse. But my friends just laugh, and my parents tell me I am too young to know what I want to do. I have thought this over very carefully, and I am very upset and discouraged. Please help me.

DEBBIE, AGE 14, NORTH CAROLINA

A **Don't let discouraging comments** get you down! Adults tend to laugh and tease because most boys and girls change their minds continually about what they want to be when they're grown up. If you are really a determined girl, time will prove it. Realizing that, you should be able to take the teasing lightly.

There is no reason to be discouraged at this early stage. But remember that to reach your goal, you must have certain abilities and be willing to accept the hard and unpleasant features of the work. Are you keen about science, for one thing? Are you reliable about duties, no matter how boring or routine? Have you inquired to see if you can take on volunteer or nurse's aide duty in a hospital during summer vacations? Are you steadily gaining in the ability to control your temper or your tears? These are just a few of the things necessary to succeed in the highly useful career you've set your heart on.

Q **This may sound ridiculous,** but it has been my desire ever since I can remember to

be an actress. I am taking piano and cello lessons, paying for the piano lessons with my movie money and getting the cello lessons free. I have taken dancing lessons but can't afford to now, and haven't managed to earn any money though I've tried hard to do so. I read books on the drama. I have won several prizes for my dancing at clubs and at school. I know acting is hard work, but I want to try. What I need to know now is whether I'm equipped to learn to be an actress.
BRENDA, AGE 12, NEW JERSEY

A **It's far from ridiculous, Brenda,** to have an ambition to make something of yourself. Having a goal, and the drive and self-confidence to push ahead, are as necessary as talent to achieve anything worth while.

Of course, you know that it is too early to determine whether you are equipped to be an actress. So far, it would seem that you are doing very well. Keep working at it—try out for dramatic productions at school, continue with your music, read plays, study speech and diction if they are taught in your school. Above all, give your talents time to develop and mature.

I think you should also try to allow a little more time for your classwork. Your letter shows that you are weak in spelling. How about concentrating on this and any other subjects that need improvement? Such training and self-discipline would be an asset to any actress-to-be. No matter what career you choose later on, you will be a more interesting and successful person with a broad background in many subjects. By doing well each day in what you are responsible for on that day, you will equip yourself for the future.

Q I haven't been baby-sitting very long, but already I've run up against something I need help with. The parents sometimes forget to pay me, or else they seem to think if they don't mention it, I won't. How can I remind them without being rude? I'm not there just for the money, and I don't want them to get the wrong impression. Please give me some advice. LYNDA, AGE 14, INDIANA

A   When the parents for whose children
you take on responsibility unintentionally forget to pay you, they won't think it's impolite
of you to remind them of the money you have
earned.

Try looking pointedly at a clock or wrist
watch and say, "Let's see. I got here at seven,
and it's now eleven . . ." Hopefully, you may
not have to go further than that before they
are handing you your well-earned fee. If they
don't get the point, you can continue with . . .
"that means you owe me . . ." And, of course,
it's always a good idea, Lynda, to have a definite understanding about what your fee is before you take the job.

Q   I am bothered about how to go about
getting babysitting jobs. The other girls I
know always seem to get them. I am friendly
toward the children in the new housing development I live in, and I have a good reputation. There should be many opportunities.
But I don't know if I should ask people di-
rectly for jobs. If it is all right to do that, how

can I approach some of the many families that have young children and babies?
Sharon, Age 13, New York

A   First of all, Sharon, you need your mother's permission. Find out if she will let you accept evening jobs, or whether you must confine your care of children to daytime hours.

Once you have a clear idea as to what she'll allow you to do, take some little 3″ by 5″ cards or slips of paper, and, in your best handwriting, write your name, address, and phone number; also the hours during which you'll be permitted to serve neighborhood parents. If you can get a friend or neighbor for whom you have "sat" to let you put down her name as a reference, add that and her phone number. When you begin making calls on people to present your cards, take pains to go at hours when housewives are not at their busiest. Even so, take up as little of their time as possible, but visit long enough to let them see you are a well-mannered girl who gives the impression of being able to handle responsibility.

Q   **My problem has two parts.** First, I am ugly. To put it straight out, I have a huge nose and protruding teeth. Much as I try to forget myself, I see my face when I do my hair, and then I think of how others have to see it all the time. Sometimes I cry myself to sleep, after a particularly nasty remark about my appearance, but I try not to let others see how I feel.

The other part of my problem is that I long to act, and have been told by my drama teacher that I have talent. It's not that I am ambitious to be a Marilyn Monroe, but with my face it's hopeless for me to think at all of acting. I am a fortunate girl in many ways, but I dread parties and affairs when I should be having a good time.

MYRNA, AGE 14, NEW ZEALAND

A   **One thing your letter didn't mention:** Is something being done about your teeth? Wearing braces for a year or so might make an immense difference not only in your appearance but in the health of your teeth. From what you say, I judge your family is able to do many things for you. If your nose is *really* as bad as you think, it might be possible that plastic surgery could correct its shape. During adolescence, before one's features become fully mature, it's very common for both boys and girls to imagine that their noses, chins, mouths are beyond endurance.

As for acting, a friend to whom I spoke about your letter, who has trained many girls for stage and television, said, "Pretty girls are a dime a dozen! What we're after is girls with talent, who are willing to work hard and who have imagination."

Stop and think a minute. Some of our greatest actresses are far from beautiful— Helen Hayes, for instance, or Judith Anderson. It's the animation that radiates from the face of an actress that makes her charming, and her voice, which she has trained to chill or thrill audiences.

You are too intelligent a girl to let surface imperfections stand in the way of your success.

I know you won't stop with merely "wishing" for you know it's "working" that's at the bottom of achievement.

Q My problem may sound trivial, but I am serious about wanting to act and don't know where to begin. I'm a sophomore in high school. I've loved acting ever since I was in pigtails (in kindergarten I was the "ham" in our little skits). I've acted since then in plays in Sunday school and other things of that type. But now that I'm thinking seriously about acting, I'd like some advice on where to start. I'd appreciate a reply very much.
FLORENCE, AGE 15, NEW YORK

A The best way to make a beginning toward any career Florence, is to do your very best in school. The broader your general understanding, the better actress you will become. *Without neglecting your other studies,* concentrate on areas relating to your chosen career, such as speech arts, literature (especially plays), good posture, and modern dance.

Acting in school plays, learning to paint scenery, typing scripts, making costumes—*whatever* you find to do—will all be preparing you for the next step toward your goal. That goal may even change in the next few years; but what you are learning to do *well* will help, no matter what your aim is.